ACTIVISM AND SOCIAL CHANGE

ACTIVISM AND SOCIAL CHANGE

LESSONS FOR COMMUNITY AND LOCAL ORGANIZING

ERIC SHRAGGE

broadview press

National Library of Canada Cataloguing in Publication

Shragge, Eric, 1948–
Activism and social change : lessons for community and local organizing /
Eric Shragge.

Includes bibliographical references and index.

ISBN 1-55111-562-X

1. Community organization. 2. Social action. I. Title.

HM831.S53 2003   361.8   C2003-903551-4

Broadview Press Ltd. is an independent, international publishing house, incorporated in 1985. Broadview believes in shared ownership, both with its employees and with the general public; since the year 2000 Broadview shares have traded publicly on the Toronto Venture Exchange under the symbol bdp.

We welcome comments and suggestions regarding any aspect of our publications—please feel free to contact us at the addresses below or at broadview@broadviewpress.com.

North America
PO Box 1243, Peterborough, Ontario, Canada K9J 7H5
3576 California Road, Orchard Park, NY, USA 14127
Tel: (705) 743-8990; Fax: (705) 743-8353
email: customerservice@broadviewpress.com

UK, Ireland, and continental Europe
Plymbridge Distributors Ltd.
Estover Road
Plymouth, PL6 7PY, UK
Tel: (01752) 202301; Fax: (01752) 202333
email: orders@plymbridge.com

Australia and New Zealand
UNIREPS, University of New South Wales
Sydney, NSW, 2052
Tel: 61 2 9664 0999; Fax: 61 2 9664 5420
email: info.press@unsw.edu.au

www.broadviewpress.com

Broadview Press Ltd. gratefully acknowledges the financial support of the Government of Canada through the Book Publishing Industry Development Program for our publishing activities.

 This book is printed on acid-free paper containing 30% post-consumer fibre.

Eco-Logo certified.
30 % Post.   PRINTED IN CANADA

CONTENTS

ACKNOWLEDGMENTS

I wrote this book as a reflection on and analysis of my many years of involvement in community organization, social movements, and local activism. As an academic, with one foot in the world of social activism, I am in a privileged position. On the university side, unlike many who live in the "ivory tower," I have been fortunate to work alongside many devoted and courageous workers in community organizations. Those who have continued the struggle for social and economic justice over many years have inspired me. Being in a university, I have had the luxury of writing, reading, and teaching about local organizing. Each part has enriched the other.

During the writing of this book, I left the School of Social Work at McGill University and joined the School of Community and Public Affairs at Concordia. I thank new colleagues for their warm welcome.

The most important group to thank are the activists I interviewed and whose voices make Chapter 5 come alive. In these interviews, I met an extraordinary group of people, who were willing to share their stories. I continue to work with some of them. It is always enriching.

Finally, thanks to Michael Harrison of Broadview Press for encouraging this project and to Betsy Struthers for her excellent editing. The book, because of it, will be far easier for you, the reader, to get through!

CHAPTER ONE

LOOKING BACK: LESSONS AND ISSUES

INTRODUCTION

Community organizing has been a central part of my life for more than 30 years. On some days, I feel that I have reached an understanding of what it is and what can be accomplished through it; on others, the uncertainties are nagging. I have been involved in many different roles, campaigns, projects, and organizations. It would be easy to idealize these experiences and to argue that community organizing has made an important contribution towards changing the fabric of North American society, but I am not a simple promoter. I have moved between periods of optimism and profound pessimism about the role of the community movement and what it has and what it can accomplish. "Accomplish" implies a normative stance. What do I mean by that? Perhaps this is the central question for this book: how does one judge what community organizing should be trying to do? The answer depends on where one stands, since that dictates what types of questions and definitions one uses and what values and political traditions shape those questions.

This chapter acts as a launching pad for a reflection on and a critical discussion of community organizing. The book itself looks backwards and forward to capture the traditions and meaning of organizing practice, starting with my experiences beginning in the late 1960s and then widening the lens. In this chapter, I will discuss my own development and experiences of practice, using autobiography in order to raise the questions and issues that shape the rest of the book. The examples that I draw upon will illustrate some of the diversity of these issues and will be a means of entering into the debates and lessons.

Although I have been teaching at a university for more than 25 years, I hope this book will depart from academic traditions. While drawing on useful academic sources, I will always come back to the politics of practice, referring to the key question of the role of community organizing in promoting and participating in the process of progressive social change. (I will avoid specific and narrow definitions of these terms for the moment.) In general, I believe that the process that leads to social change begins when large numbers of people act collectively in their own self-interest to promote economic and social justice. In the process of working for these ideals, it is necessary and, indeed, equally important to expand democratic opportunities and increase the control of people over the institutions that effect their lives. In other words, political and social ends are defined by material gains and changing relations of power. Perhaps this is too idealistic a position for our pragmatic world of partnership and deal-making, but it is the starting point for me and will act as a crude benchmark for later discussions.

Why have I decided to write this book now? There are two answers, one easy, the other more complex. The easy one is that I began this project on sabbatical leave when writing this book seemed like a good project to undertake. The real and deeper answer is that I feel out of step with many of the practices and beliefs found in community organizations today. This is not a recent feeling, but has been building for many years. I was shaped by the ideals of the 1960s and the political and social analyses and perspectives that grew out of that period. I have witnessed the changes in the community movement since then. There are some positive developments, but, at the same time, there has been a loss of the movement's critical edge and engagement in the wider struggle for economic and social justice. Also, while social conditions have deteriorated for many, community organizations have become part of the system—part of the problem—rather than a source of opposition to the forces that have reshaped the economy and social life. This book examines the changes in the movement and the forces that have led to its redefinition as a way to learn lessons from the past in order to critique the present and to find new paths on which to move forward.

I begin my discussion with some basic questions: how did I get involved in community organizing, what were the processes, and what has changed in practice over the years? On the first question, I start from a vantage-point shaped by political questions and issues. Community organizing at its best has created sites for the practice of opposition. Those interested in progressive social change and social justice were attracted to the community movement because it was a place to organize resistance to the system of global capitalism, patriarchy, racism, and other forms of socio-economic oppression and domination. They believed that the local community—the neighbourhood—was a place where people could meet to challenge those forces that oppressed them and, in the process, learn about the relationship of personal issues to the wider forces that shaped them. Thus, forms of collective action were seen to be the products of the meeting of the personal and the political. Although this is a simplification for the motive for and results of community action, this belief was, and is, at its core. People may be interested in community for a variety of other reasons, but I felt, and feel, that participation in local activities is for the purpose of building opposition. I am not only talking about protest and confrontation, but the creation of democratic opportunities through which people can learn about their collective strengths and build social solidarity. In the community, there are a variety of practices that may not seem oppositional, but which do question relations of power, build alternative visions, and shift power to those who usually do not have it. In other words, working in the community sector is a political opportunity. It is one that can be taken and used to promote social change.

My interest in community organizing, however, is not only political, but personal. I came from a secure middle-class home with professional parents, who valued success for their children in traditional terms. Nonetheless, my orientation has been unambiguously on the left, the non-traditional, libertarian left influenced by both Marxists and anarchists. There are not many out there with me anymore, and my viewpoint does not often find itself expressed in the corporate-dominated media. More to the point, I rarely see these perspectives and beliefs among those with whom I engage in political work for social change. Frankly, I am often unsure of where people stand, whether they are vague social democrats or progressive pragmatists trying to make life a little more tolerable for those on the margins. Many people from similar backgrounds were radical in their youth, but there are few that have maintained their engagement over many years.

Where did the trip start? It began, perhaps, with exposure to a tradition of social justice through synagogue affiliation and related youth movements. I have clear memories of a presentation by a young man who went to participate in the civil rights struggles in the early 1960s in the southern United States and how his promotion of non-violence was met by violence in return. I remember trying to convince a Hebrew school teacher that, based on principles of justice in Jewish traditions, communism was a more appropriate ideology than capitalism. But I had little exposure in my home to the old left of the previous generation, except through a couple of my parents' friends. On the other hand, my parents reminded my brothers and me of our privilege relative to most others. My grandparents were immigrants, and poverty was only a generation back. Another factor, perhaps, was that I did not fit in well or feel comfortable with the "in crowd." By high school I was more intellectually intense and serious than most of my peers. Sparked by the events of the 1960s, such as the civil rights and anti-war movements, I felt that something profound was happening and, by my third year at university (1968), that the world was coming undone. I participated in few protests at that time and began to learn that the radical challenge of the period had profound roots and ideas that were often lost in the culture of "turning on, tuning in, dropping out."

I fell into organizing, partly by accident, partly because of the times. During my undergraduate years studying genetics and related biological sciences at McGill between 1965 and 1969, the universities exploded with student activism. I was involved only peripherally, as a member of a group of Jewish students who challenged the priorities of their community and who got a hearing by threatening to disrupt a Passover service at a rich Westmount synagogue. I was also involved with a group that demanded student representation on Genetics Department committees. Looking back, however, it is the images rather than social understanding and knowledge that I remember most: a long-haired, bearded male student seated in a university board of governor's chair during an occupation; the snowballs thrown by engineering students at a large group (of which I was one) protesting the firing of a left-wing, activist, political science teacher. By the late 1960s, the campus was theatre; the key campaign was against the United States' war in Vietnam, while the local issue was demands for an extension of democracy with parity of students on university committees and decision-making bodies. We argued that universities had to be part of a critical reflection on the injustices in society and, therefore, part of the opposition to corporate capitalism.

I felt pulled by the excitement of the period, the sense of social optimism that social change and justice were possible. We believed as a generation that we would make a major contribution to that process. During that time, I was involved in the Jewish community, working at a synagogue and at the YM-YWHA (Young Men's-Young Women's Hebrew Association) as a youth worker as well with teens at a summer camp. By 1968, I had decided that I wanted a career in social work. It wasn't a difficult decision, since my grades in my genetics courses were mediocre, and I had lost interest in chasing fruit flies around a laboratory or doing genetic counselling. Besides, the world was changing, and I wanted to be part of it. I knew very little about social work, but thought it would allow me to make a positive contribution to society. So off I went to the University of Michigan in Ann Arbor to become a social worker. I was naive and had a strong sense of both right and wrong and social justice, but I was a political illiterate. I had no sense of the traditions of the left that would play such an important part in my life. My education in the biological sciences at McGill left me with little in the way of tools for social analysis. Somehow, the challenges to authority and the questioning of the legitimacy of the social order helped shape my identity, and I began to see myself as a radical, to use the jargon of the period. I don't think I knew what that meant, except as a visceral antagonism to major social and economic institutions. If asked at the time, I don't think I would have placed myself on the left. To me, the left meant either social democrats and/or pro-Soviet Union communists, neither of which had any appeal to me then or now.

My political formation and definition as an activist really began in the School of Social Work at the University of Michigan. I entered immediately after my undergraduate degree, leaving home for the first time for an extended period. My previous experiences had not prepared me for the two years that followed. My first field placement was in an inner city school; as well, I volunteered with both a local tenants' union to support a large successful rent strike and with a centre for street kids; during the summer, with a few others, I participated in a recruiting drive for a welfare rights organization. I met people who legitimated, for me, the necessity both for radical social change and my desire to be part of it. It was not always easy. I felt intimidated by more experienced and knowledgeable activists, but felt better as I began to find my place. I became more confident about my own identity as a radical, as someone who was trying to find a way to live a life that made social change activities central to it. I wanted to pursue a career as a community organizer, and I decided that mainstream social work was not for me. I was fortunate, because it was a period in which community organizing had legitimacy in the profession.

As part of this reflection, I want to recall images of that period to convey its spirit, not as a process of glorification of the past, but rather in an attempt to describe my experiences in more than one dimension. Keeping in mind that the goal of this exercise is to understand the present, these images, as well as ideas, will help. For instance,

I remember some of the welfare recipients, their strength to not only survive but to challenge the oppression of poverty in the United States. One white woman, a welfare rights activist whose wrists were scarred from suicide attempts, was a community leader and, along with a Black friend, staged sit-ins in several churches throughout Ann Arbor to demand reparations for the churches' support of slavery. Courage was necessary. The year before I arrived for graduate school, the local sheriff had called out the dogs to attack a peaceful demonstration of welfare mothers. During my field placement in an inner city school in Detroit, a Black youngster eight or ten years old told me about hiding under his bed while tanks drove down his street in the aftermath of the great race riots of the time. On campus, the Black Action Movement shut down the university for more than a week in a strike that demanded increased admissions and support for Black students. I remember getting up at five in the morning to picket the university heating plant because the union said that it would not cross a picket line. Heavy wet snow, rain, and slush did not deter us. It was an important lesson for me about the necessity of links between organized labour and social movements. Also, I learned about the power of numbers to disrupt and shut institutions and to win concessions through this process.

This is how we understood what we referred to then as "Amerika." Polarization in society was real: white kids were busted for simple possession of illegal drugs; Black Panthers faced police who had declared war on them; some young men went to jail or fled the country to avoid the draft; and the anti-authoritarian youth culture did not know its left from its right. One of the first and most important lessons I learned was that I was an outsider, despite what I believed and the solidarity I could offer. I was not poor, but white, privileged, and educated, with many potential life choices. As I became more active over the years that followed, I learned that trust was something that had to be earned. It came with time, respect, and a willingness to listen and to act in support and not to take over when it seemed to me that I knew better than those with whom I was working. Thus, there was always tension in the relationship. I learned that people like myself may bring skills, knowledge, and a useful status to a group or a struggle, but at the same time we have to know our place and the reason we are there: to help build a true democracy in which people can have control and a voice. This was an early and important lesson for me.

Thus began my political education. I came to believe that opposition to established powers and values was necessary. I found that solidarity with people working together for a common cause was fundamentally moving. And I experienced the playing out of social conflict as a "high." These experiences were not unique, and I was in no way central. I remained on the margins, did my bit, and learned profound lessons. I knew that there was something in community organizing that could link my emerging political consciousness with a way to express it. All seemed possible—with the right combination of commitment and moral fiber, we could accomplish anything.

Over the years, I have found many ways to stay involved, such as organizing neighbourhoods and being active in the peace movement. I will describe a few of these and examine some of the questions they raised and the lessons I learned from them. Other practice experiences will be studied in the chapters that follow. Here, I present a critical reflection of the kind that has shaped much scholarship and which has grown from experiences in the field and analysis of that practice.

NEIGHBOURHOOD ORGANIZING

In 1974, I was hired by the School of Social Work at McGill University as a field instructor, mandated to develop field placements for students in the community and to supervise their work there. The school had already developed a placement with a small recreation association in a working-class area. The housing was three-floor, walk-up apartment buildings hastily built after World War II; although privately owned, they were subsidized through long-term, low-interest mortgages provided through a federal government housing program. I think the small group who ran the recreation association and those at the School of Social Work expected me to put in place a tutorial service and an after-school program for children and youth. I was, however, strongly influenced by Saul Alinsky, an American community organizer (more on him in Chapter 3), and wanted to organize people to take on issues such as housing and neighbourhood conditions that affected their lives. Besides, I was supervising six students who were keen to try something different. So we embarked on a period of intense door-knocking, speaking to as many residents as we could. The issues identified were typical: lack of repairs in apartments, unsafe conditions in the alleys, etc. We brought small groups together, meeting in peoples' homes or in the recreation centre, which was situated in a small basement apartment. We got people to move into action; we won some concessions and made a bit of a name for ourselves. The first landlord we took on was a prominent physician. In order to get him to negotiate, tenants picketed his house in an upper-class neighbourhood and walked into his clinic. These events were covered in the media, and these actions finally brought him to the negotiating table with his lawyer in tow. He agreed to the demands of the tenants but subsequently sold his property. These activities created tension with those in charge of the recreation centre, who were connected to the government of the city and indirectly to the mayor, Jean Drapeau. However, despite their opposition, there was enough support to create an independent neighbourhood organization called POWER (Peoples' Organization of Westhaven Elmhurst Residents).

In addition to this work, I was fortunate to be affiliated with the Parallel Institute, an organizing centre in Pointe St. Charles, a working-class district with a tradition of activism. The organizing staff at Parallel had recently broadened their mandate from welfare rights to neighbourhood organizing. For several years, my students and I worked with Parallel as it established organizations in other working-class communities. All of these organizing drives achieved concrete gains, improving housing, municipal services, and other conditions. In addition, organizers identified local leaders and trained them to play public and active roles in the development of the organizations. The structures were based on committees formed on city blocks, which were then joined together to form the larger group. However, all of the organizers and some of the leaders recognized the limits of local work. A couple of campaigns were based on common issues such as the City of Montreal's refusal to post and enforce 20-mile-an-hour zones around parks and schools and the lack of beat police. These were relatively successful; the coalition of local organizations forced the city to make concessions. Disruptive tactics, such as the occupation of a City-owned restaurant and confrontations with high-ranking officials, were significant actions in these campaigns. The key element was the mobilization of large numbers of people. This was not only an important aspect of the work, but the central principle, one that has been forgotten by many community workers and their organizations today.

Larger campaigns, such as challenging the rate structures and other policies of the natural gas and hydro-electric companies, were envisioned. The idea behind these was to enlarge the base of the organizing and to bring representatives from other groups to these actions. We were not successful in achieving these goals. There was suspicion among French-speaking popular organizations, who had developed a different style and priorities, and other more conventional groups, like those representing older people, who did not invest a lot of energy in these actions. The failure of these campaigns and an impatience with the limits of local work to get at some of the basic class and broader social questions led to a gradual abandonment of these efforts. The group that I had organized went through other incarnations and continued to operate for several years after my departure.

These experiences contributed many positive lessons and raised some questions. On the positive side, I learned about the potential in and the difficulties of working in grassroots organizing. I had to start from scratch in the neighbourhood and train students to do the work. One of the first things they had to learn was that they were not doing social work in any of the ways they were being taught. They were out there, at peoples' doors, to promote an idea of social change through participation in a local organizing effort. Individual change (casework) was not part of the program. Once they got that idea, it was easier to move ahead. The process was to use the discontent residents felt and to channel it into organizing. There was always a tension between what people felt and what they were willing to do.

Perhaps it was the times (mid-1970s) and the actual conditions that contributed to the willingness of people to invite you into their homes and discuss problems; however, this did not necessarily translate into action. Sometimes a student would tell me that he/she had talked to many people on a block and expected to see 25 of them at the first meeting. Usually, only five or six showed up.

Willingness to participate in local action was affected by a variety of factors, such as people's energy levels and time commitments— shift work, child care, etc. Many believed that nothing could be accomplished, and others hoped that they could move out of the neighbourhood. Further, gender shaped the organizing effort. The neighbourhood was viewed as an extension of the home, and the issues tended to attract more women than men. For women taking on a public persona as a leader created tensions at home, and their activities were at times discouraged by their husbands. The process of mobilization was difficult; it took time and investment in people. But it was possible and did, sometimes, succeed. This is the lesson I still carry. Mobilization is a key element; without it, there is little an organization can do. There are two good reasons for this. First, the power of an organization to win issues is built on the number of people involved actively within it. Second, in the process of participating in local struggle, people gain awareness, form solidarity with others, and create democratic opportunities. Community organizing can contribute to social change by mobilizing people to act for their own interest in an organized way. The most effective efforts always occur through mobilization. Perhaps the most discouraging change in the community movement has been forgetting this. More and more, organizations represent people or at least claim that they do, but they do not try to capture the spirit that is present in the process of organizing when people speak and act on their own behalf.

CRITICAL COMMENTS AND QUESTIONS

The period of effective organizing was short, only a few years. The work was hard to sustain. It is not easy, particularly now, to find support for the type of organizing that we were doing then. Funding bodies do not like to support projects and efforts that are "political," meaning those that overtly challenge the status quo through organizing people directly. Such efforts cannot be easily controlled. Given these difficulties, we had some success. In retrospect, however, lessons can be learned by raising some critical issues.

I will discuss the essential question of organization in the chapters that follow. For now, I want to raise a doubt that bothered me even at the time. We spent a lot of time and energy on organizational maintenance. Our small neighbourhood groups often held many regular meetings every month, including block meetings, coordinating committee meetings with representatives from each block, committee meetings that were focussed on specific issues, and leadership meetings, as well as weekly meetings of the organizing team. The structure provided stability and appeared to be a democratic, transparent process of decision-making, but it took a toll. There were not many leaders, and, after a while, they were spending more time in meetings than in any other part of the process. For organizers the impact was similar. An organizer must work on recruitment. It is *the* most important task. When the demands of organizational maintenance become too great, recruitment does not occur, and the organization does not grow.

Thus, the lesson for me is that building organization requires the creation of simple, flexible structures that allow new recruits and leaders to enter. It is too easy for a stagnant organization to hide behind a stable structure. The processes we participated in were dynamic when they were working well. The tension is between putting in place an organizational form that is transparent and open versus one that takes over the time and energy of those involved for internal processes. With this experience, I have begun to believe that organizing is more about short-term initiatives rather than long-term stable structures. I will return to this throughout the book, but I raise it here because I think there is a great deal of confusion about the concepts of community organization and community organizing. The latter is about a process that does not necessarily reproduce the weight of organization. Further, as one puts in place more formal organizations and structures, funds are required to pay support staff and for operating expenses. Fund-raising rather than the pursuit of its goals and mission can become the driving force of organizational life. Even in the 1970s, when securing funds for innovative activities was relatively easier, this was an issue. As organizations grew, there were greater demands for money, demands which could distort the goals of the organization either because of the time and energy devoted to these ends or because the money received was linked to the priorities of the funder and not the organization itself.

Over the years, I have thought a lot about the role of community organizers, particularly their accountability and their influence in local groups. Organizers are outsiders. I experienced this sharply in these early door-to-door encounters. I was young, educated, and male, while many who were prepared to become active had not had access to much formal education, were women with young children, or worked in menial jobs. Because of who I was, I had influence and some power. In addition, I had read books on the subject, worked in organizing before, and had a good idea of the type of work I was doing. The relationship was not equal. It took a while to build trust. Why should an organizer be trusted? We were asking people to behave differently in relations of authority—to challenge the land-lord, to fight city hall. However, now as then, organizing is not manipulation. People ultimately vote with their feet. An organizer has no rewards or benefits to give out; participation is voluntary. If residents attend meetings and participate in the process, it is because they have become convinced of the merits of the work and because they have cemented a relationship with the organizer.

Having argued this, it is also important to acknowledge that organizers have power to shape agendas and pick and support lead-ers. I have come to believe that there is little one can do about this relationship. Community organizers do facilitate and stimulate local processes that would not have happened otherwise. It is important, however, to acknowledge their roles and their power. The relation-ship between organizers and the organization changes over time. In the beginning, it is usually the organizer who has a lot of power. As the organization matures, with a structure put in place, the role of the organizer should shift and become more like that of a staff member accountable to the membership. This shift is central and should allow leaders and members to strengthen their voice. The role of the organizer and her/his power and role are inevitable, and the difficult questions they raise need to be confronted. They are not easily resolved. If a community organization is, in practice, democratic, a place in which active participation of its members can become a possibility, then organizers have to learn both to live with the tensions around their own power and authority and to actively shift control to members and leaders.

Another question that troubled me at the time was the relationship of this type of neighbourhood organizing to wider processes of social change. By the end of the 1970s, there was a strong Marxist-Leninist movement in Quebec. There were major divisions in this movement with several Maoist tendencies. These political groups had attracted many young, politicized activists, who brought their politics into factories and the community movement. Drawing on the legacy of Marxism, they not only promoted but actively pushed the level of class analysis; however, their style and authoritarian form of organization alienated many of the working class they were trying to recruit. For me, although I accepted their analysis along with some of the Marxist scholarly work that was being revisited in the university, I rejected their authoritarianism. In some ways, Marxist analysis helped to clarify how class interest shaped relations in capitalist society. The Parallel Institute group believed that we were organizing people in the English-speaking working class, who would participate in a wider working-class revolution in Quebec. In retrospect, this is certainly naïve and inaccurate. Further, the people we were organizing did not buy any of it. They were able to understand interest and power, how these relations affected them in their neighbourhoods and workplaces, and how capitalism created poverty and unhealthy living conditions. But they did not believe in the rhetoric of the "far left." They wanted the concrete and local gains that can be made through organizing—better housing and neighbourhood conditions.

From a Marxist perspective, primary class contradictions are played out in factories, through the struggles at the point of production. Work in the community is secondary. These ideas created doubt for me about the potential of local work. What was the role of community organizing as a way of promoting social change? The way I try to answer this question has remained relatively consistent over the years. Fundamentally, the core for me is power and who has it; organizing is the means of creating a collective voice and allowing a group to shape events that touch their lives. There is a danger here, and this is one challenge that Marxism raised. What is this voice for? Is it necessarily progressive? Does it ally itself with working-class and, later, feminist struggles? Here the answer is no. We have certainly seen right-wing groups using the lessons of organizing to promote their position and to make demands on the state. There has to be another dimension—ideology and/or values— and here we are treading on a path strewn with obstacles. The organizing that I did was shaped by values such as increasing social and economic equality and extending democracy. But we live in a society that teaches that inequality is inevitable and deserved and that most people are so uninformed that they really are not capable of making decisions. Further, selecting between political parties on a regular basis is what democracy is all about. The challenge is to move from day-to-day organizing to ideology without imposing the latter. The Marxists put ideology on the table and used community organizations as forums for political education, promoting their own political line while ignoring the immediate interests of the group. In some ways, this undermined the effectiveness of organizing, and, in some instances, the Marxists were kicked out. For me, what is required is a balance between maintaining concrete struggles in which people can learn to work collectively and build power and raising the broader political and social questions. The lesson of that period was that both are needed, along with a solid dose of alliance-building in order to broaden the local into a wider vision of social change.

We need to work on achieving this balance. It is the central challenge: to keep one eye on winning local, concrete struggles and the other eye on the broader picture, building bridges with the wider struggle. The organizer, as I will discuss in the next chapter, has to understand that, for people to be involved in local work, there has to be something in it for them. At the same time, he/she has an educational role to play that goes beyond the immediate experience to wider social and political movements. I will now turn to an experience with a broader social movement in order to see the type of politics that were missing in local work; in the process, I will indirectly contrast organizing processes.

PEACE MOVEMENT ACTIVITIES

The early and mid-1980s was a period of intense activity in the peace and disarmament movement. The United States had raised the stake in the nuclear arms race along with its rhetoric against the Soviet Union. Not to be outdone, the latter became a weaker mirror image of the former. The two at times seemed to be in an irrational death struggle with most of humanity as collateral damage. The most dramatic events did not involve the super powers with their positioning and escalation, but the massive opposition to them. I will not enter into an analysis of the arms race and the politics of the period, but it forms a backdrop for very important personal and political lessons about the role of organizing within a social movement and some of the challenges and opportunities that were provided through that experience. Further, as I will argue in the next chapter, there is a continuity between these movements and those that organized the mobilization in Seattle in 1999 and other similar opposition against globalization and free trade.

I became active in the peace movement through my connection with the magazine *Our Generation*, which had its origins in the 1960s in the movement for nuclear disarmament. Through one of its editors, I became a member of a group called Academics for Nuclear Disarmament, which had produced a statement alerting the public to the dangers of the arms race. I found that, typical of the peace movement, there were many people with good intentions but little skill or capacity for the organization of public protest and mobilization. At the same time, there was a strong public sentiment and support for disarmament. The movement brought together a variety of political traditions and orientations. In Canada, the main campaign was against Cruise missile testing. The broad-based movement did not stop the testing, but did discredit the use of nuclear weapons and challenged the premise of the East/West divide of the Cold War. Thus, as opposed to community organizations that work for specific gains, social movements do not have their impact in that limited way. Rather, they change popular understanding of the area of their campaigns; they redefine commonsense understanding of the issues.

The period was a rich one for me. I was involved with a wide variety of groups working in the disarmament movement, and there was a positive and exciting energy. I was proud of my part in organizing a large disarmament demonstration—an estimated 30,000 people formed a human chain between the Soviet and the United States consulates in Montreal. Such demonstrations did not always translate into effectiveness, but were a point of convergence for many political actors, ranging from feminists, ecologists, and trade unionists to a variety of lefties of all stripes. This type of convergence was rare, but joining together for common campaigns created a climate of optimism and a space for politics that could be done differently. There were, however, divisions. On the tactical side, there were those who believed that civil disobedience and getting arrested was the only morally legitimate tactic, while others wanted to appeal to a majority who would be attracted to more traditional means of protest. Ideologically, there were divisions between those who supported the Soviet Union and groups such as the one I was working with that argued for a policy of non-alignment. There were those who wanted the positions of the peace movement to be shaped by a more radical ideology and a long-term vision of social change and those who saw it as a single issue. These were some of the complexities. For this discussion, it is the lessons for community organizing that are important.

The significant contrast for me between community organization and the peace movement is the form of organization. The former tends to involve a clear structure with specific roles for staff and volunteers. While there are peace and disarmament organizations, the movement is, by definition, decentralized with many centres of activity. Spontaneity of action in unexpected places creates the sense of movement. Also, the way the issues and actions touch people in places where there is no specific organization contributes to its breadth and convergence. For example, teachers have brought peace issues into the classroom, unionists have talked about converting military facilities to civilian production, women have organized peace camps, and students and professors have confronted issues of military research on campuses. Can this type of convergence be consciously reproduced or is it a reaction to specific events? I believe that these moments are important, but they cannot be "organized." Rather, they come about because of small efforts in many places to keep ideas alive, sustain action in general, and bring new analysis of events to public awareness. In the beginning, the peace movement was not a spontaneous departure. It grew out of other social and political movements. Its success reflected how these had achieved a sophisticated organizational capacity and readiness to engage with a wider public. As I will argue in the next chapter, such activities and perspectives have continued. Each new round of activity contributes positive and negative lessons about how to go forward to the next round of struggle.

Trusting diversity and decentralization are key elements to such growth. In community organization, we are taught to put together tightly organized events. The peace movement did that. For example, the human chain described above was the product of many months of planning, mobilization, and education. At the same time, many events and new forms of activity sprang up in unaffiliated groups. Such forms are by definition loose and chaotic. Attempts at centralization often occur after the blossoming of the local and usually fail as the local forms demobilize. I was part of a group that tried to put together a province-wide organization of non-aligned peace groups, but it never came to much. The activity centres represented by these groups were event-specific and did not have long-term expectations and agendas. By the time a broad-based organization was put in place, the peak of the mobilization and popular support had passed, and meetings became routine, providing little in the way of excitement and energy. There is a delicate balance between the necessity of coordination and imposing an organizational form on movement activities. This was an important lesson for me and supports my belief that large mobilizations are short-term and cannot be shaped by traditional types of organization. One has to go with the energy of the movement, bring into it political perspectives, and contribute to building alliances, but the movement will run its course. I think that in community organizing, we spend too much time on putting structures in place and too little time on the actions that create and support a spirit of movement and opposition.

Practices of working by consensus were important elements in the peace movement process. We did not only oppose a range of issues related to peace, but we did it in ways that challenged hierarchy and domination. The most overt practice was consensus decision-making, which came to us mainly from the women's movement. There was conflict about this practice. Some argued in a principled way for it, while others did not want to waste time on the arduous process of building consensus. I participated in many meetings, which were slowed by the difficult process of arriving at decisions we all were able to accept. A vote would have been faster, but those on the losing side would not have had their voices heard in the same way. I liked the process but saw some flaws in it. Consensus decision-making implies that those participating in the decision have a shared core of beliefs. Decisions, therefore, are premised on common assumptions. Consensus can work in situations in which there is openness to working out an agreement on specific aspects of the work, as long as these do not compromise core values; yet, in broad-based *ad hoc* arrangements such as the peace movement, core beliefs are seldom discussed. Consensus is difficult when people from diverse political and social backgrounds come together to organize a specific event or campaign.

We experimented with process in other ways. In public meetings, women remarked that men spoke more frequently than they did. In order to ameliorate this situation, we passed a rule that men and women speakers would alternate, particularly in public meetings. This did have a positive effect and reduced the dominant role that men often played in these forums. Affinity groups as a means to prepare for direct action were part of wider campaigns; these were small groups who trained together for an act of non-violent civil disobedience, such as occupying or blocking entrances to government and/or corporate offices. Actions were prepared through coordination between these groups, which were democratically organized and worked on the principles of consensus decision-making. It was not only the way the affinity groups functioned that interested me, but the way they created a decentralized approach to direct action. Drawing on Mahatma Gandhi's principles of non-violence, the tradition goes back to many different campaigns and has extended into the present in the protests against the corporate world order and globalization. The key lesson here is how the process is intertwined with outcomes. Social movements of our time implicitly challenge the limits of parliamentary democracy and argue that a broader voice has to be heard. However, at the same time, new democratic practices need to be constructed so that the process of building protest in practice includes the voices of those involved and reduces the influence of traditional forms of leadership.

Perhaps the most important lesson of the peace movement has been the complex interaction of the global and the local. The slogan "think globally, act locally" now sounds little more than a cliché. In fact, it was the key element in the new practice that paved the way for the contemporary social movements against globalization. The escalation of the arms race was a problem far removed from the neighbourhoods and the institutions in which we organized. At the local level, for example, I was part of a neighbourhood group that conducted an independent popular referendum to declare our district a nuclear free zone. We had no formal authority and what we did had no legal weight, but we reached hundreds of people through education and the voting itself, and were part of a larger coalition that pressured the City of Montreal into declaring itself nuclear free. These gestures were largely symbolic, but created the momentum for a larger challenge.

At the same time as the work was going on "from below," new forms of international networking were taking place. Internationalism built on the momentum of local action and stimulated it as well. I was fortunate to attend a European Nuclear Disarmament conference in Amsterdam in 1985. There were activists from all over Europe and America building their analyses and sharing strategies in an atmosphere of solidarity. The events they described and proposed demonstrated the necessity of linking the local with the global in ways that were concrete and specific. I was witnessing internationalism in practice. Some of the renewed activism confronting the processes of globalization today is built on patterns established in the peace movement. Local autonomy, decentralized structures, and effective communication facilitate shared analysis and perspectives that contribute to the creation of internationalist practice.

When I meet people who were active in the early 1980s, we share a strong sense of personal friendship gained from doing politics in an atmosphere of personal and political solidarity in spite of the differences in our backgrounds and interests. At the same time, I do not want to idealize the experience—there were conflicts both political and personal. These are inevitable in an open movement. For most of us, the work was voluntary and intruded into our personal lives; we were required to balance jobs, childcare responsibilities, and relationships with the demands of the movement. These were part of it—learning to live your politics with the reality of your life. That challenge was one that provoked personal growth and reflection.

I also had questions and doubts. One tension for me was between my background as a community organizer and my role as a movement activist. The former teaches two things that conflict with the latter. First, an organizer tries to balance his or her ideology and values with the demands of group cohesion. Thus, almost by definition, there are compromises made. In the context of a social movement, it is more permissible and often necessary to polarize questions even if they appear to be divisive. The question of non-alignment was an example of this dilemma. Many in the peace movement had fallen into an uncomfortable alliance with pro-Soviet forces that were led internationally by the World Peace Council. Others opposed this organization for tactical and more fundamental reasons. I will not go into the arguments here except to state that we were not interested in reproducing Cold War hysteria, but we wanted to oppose the escalating, reciprocal nature of the arms race.

Another source of conflict centred around the question of support for the independent peace movements that emerged in Eastern Bloc countries. Some thought that their issues should be ignored in the interest of unity. Those of us who supported a non-aligned perspective thought that a unity that ignored their issues would be a false unity and that an alternative vision that went "beyond the blocs" was a starting point for international peace. The debate put me in a new role, as a partisan of a position and not as an organizer who pursued consensus and unity. Further, I began to feel more strongly that it was important to bring vision and explicit politics into the organizing process. There is an inevitable tension between how much and how far one can balance vision and engagement with diversity. Without vision and explicit politics, the possibility of basic social change is lost; at the same time, it is impossible to mobilize large numbers if one remains sectarian.

A second tension was between organization building versus the style and forms of organization of a social movement. Community organizing is premised on the assumption that building a relatively permanent structure with clear processes of delegation of power and roles facilitates longevity and democracy. Social movements tend to be much looser. Groups mobilize for specific campaigns or actions and then disband, although some may continue to play an educational or more traditional lobbying function. They are energized during specific periods of mass mobilization. However, it is impossible to impose a structure on a movement. Organizations can grow out of the movement, but they will not sustain a mass mobilization that is time-limited. The role of activists is to support and to contribute to specific events and campaigns, bringing critical politics and debate into them, but they cannot expect that the movement as such can be organized.

Finally, despite the reservations and questions that I have raised about neighbourhood organizing and the peace movement, I felt at the time of my early involvement that the spirit of these activities was optimistic. The revolution did not happen, but there were victories: new leadership was supported, political consciousness was promoted, and, in general, there was a sense that social change was possible through both neighbourhood and social movement organizing. However, in the years that followed, the context shifted. I had been outside of community organizations for several years and, by the mid-to-late 1980s when I returned, I noticed many changes had taken place. These were not positive, and in some ways, as I will elaborate, they were the impetus for this book.

CHANGING DIRECTION: COMMUNITY ORGANIZING REDEFINED

When I returned to community organizing in the mid-1980s, I discovered that the context and the debate had shifted. First, unemployment had risen in a way unprecedented since the Great Depression of the 1930s, and de-industrialization had become a fact of life for many cities. Factory closures with massive lay-offs were daily occurrences in working-class neighbourhoods. The consequences were high levels of poverty, and for many young people the possibilities of work seemed remote. The second factor was the restructuring of the role of the state. Not only was the welfare state cut back, but more fundamentally there was an ideological shift. The state would no longer be the primary social provider; the market and the community were to share the responsibility. New relationships between the community and the government were in place. Community organizations were pressured into partnership with government, and innovative solutions were sought in order to confront the crisis.

I became involved in two projects. The first was in the organizing committee for, and subsequently as a member of, the executive of a community council in my own district. The second was in community economic development (CED), which will be discussed in detail in a later chapter. Here, I will talk about some of the general shifts, why I found them discouraging, and how they may be improved. Since these themes are central to this book, I will sketch out the basic elements from a personal point of view.

The most striking shift, particularly after participating in peace movement activities, was the lack of mobilization. Community organizations represented and advocated on behalf of their members or clients. There were a few instances of attempts to mobilize, but these seemed to me to be half-hearted and not systematic. It had not been that many years before that, as organizers, we had insisted on the basic premise that one had to reach "the people," and, in order to do this, one had to spend time in their homes and other places where they congregated. Organizing was about bringing people together, helping them to have a voice, and representing their own interests. Instead, I found politically progressive professionals who believed that they could represent people without consulting with them; this, they felt, was the best path towards working for social change. In doing so, however, they lost their base and their legitimacy.

Another shift was the development of many different services by community organizations, reflecting a range of politics. Some were innovative and creative, finding experimental ways to respond to social problems (some examples will discussed in later chapters); some embodied the values and politics of the social movement activists that started them (for example, women's shelters); and some were traditional charities (for example, food banks). I will discuss these shifts in detail in Chapter 4. The point for me was that the community sector seemed to be politically at a dead-end. It had become competent and professionalized; had negotiated recognition from the government; and, in many instances, had secured recurring funding arrangements. The relationship with the state was complex and unclear. On the one hand, there was an element of conflict over the status of these new services and other social policies; on the other, there was collaboration and new partnership between government and community. One thing was sure: there was little at the grassroots, as community organizations stood between the people and the state in a kind of mediating or advocating relationship. I saw this relationship played out in the community council. It became an organization of organizations. We campaigned for improvements and contributed to some, such as the building of a swimming pool and an enlarged recreation centre. However, in those campaigns, public meetings were rare, and the leadership fell into the hands of professionals.

Another new form came in vogue in this period—Community Economic Development (CED). I fell into it, rather than seeking it out. It seemed to me that the integration of economic development into the community had potential, since I believed that the split between the social and the economic had been one of the limits of community organizing. For 10 years I was a member of various Boards of Directors and working groups in CED organizations; as well, through research projects and writing, I was able to learn a lot about it. I maintained a critical stance, acknowledging its limited potential for social change, but recognizing at the same time its enormous danger. Like any other community project, its potential was its ability to create democratic opportunities and to help people find ways to gain power. The danger was the ideology it promoted, along with its government funders and representatives of big business— that small-scale and individual enterprise was a solution to the growing crisis of work. Some CED was initiated at the local level through coalitions of social actors such as community, unions, and business as a way to respond to the economic devastation of the 1980s. In Montreal, after several of these grassroots efforts had gained a foothold and received funding, the city, provincial, and federal governments saw using them as a useful strategy to promote local economic development. In addition, the established organizations became para-governmental with narrow definitions of their mandates. In some ways, these organizations set up new ruling relations at the local level as they administered pre-packaged government programs, particularly those aimed at integrating the unemployed into the labour market. I witnessed these changes, and, within one of the organizations, I pushed for a strategy that would be more active in the promotion of an economic vision for the district, including public hearings. These never happened because the leadership of the organization would not step out of the pre-determined program packages imposed by their funding agencies. I am discouraged by these processes and feel that CED practice in Montreal has been rapidly institutionalized.

However, I do recognize the potential in the CED movement, particularly in grassroots initiatives that organize democratic workplaces. Some CED organizations promote alternative perspectives on local development to take into account low-cost housing, job creation, and public participation in the process. It is the underlying belief in small business development, the entrepreneurial spirit, that I question the most. In some CED organizations, there is little promotion of a collective vision. Effort is put into organizing support for business development, such as access to credit and technical resources. I have described this as "trickle sideways," as there are few benefits except to a small group who sets up the business. At the same time, it promotes an ideology that small business development can compensate for high levels of poverty. I do not believe it; it is like using micro-tools to fix macro-problems. I decided that, because of the emphasis on small business development, its technocratic/administrative face, and most important its lack (with a couple of exceptions) of engagement with the wider community in a political and social process, I would leave the board and executive of the CED organization.

The period of the 1980s and 1990s created a community sector with a professionally controlled service orientation rather than a community movement. It had become for me an outgrowth of the state with little autonomy or vision of social change. I was out of step, and often in meetings I felt profoundly alienated. I had seen community organizing go from "adolescence," with anger, hope, and energy, to "adulthood," which meant compliance and acceptance of a "responsible" social role within the social order. There were ongoing challenges and continuity with the more contentious past, but these were in the minority and did not have much success in mobilizing citizens.

ATTEMPTS AT RENEWAL

In 1998, I returned to grassroots neighbourhood organizing. It was an experience that, for a while, renewed optimism about the prospect for community organizing. An old friend approached me to help him with a new organizing initiative in a low-income, multicultural neighbourhood in Montreal. I won't go into all of the details and all of the mistakes and problems (there were many!), but I will start with the positive highlights. The main attraction for me was the commitment to a grassroots process that would mobilize people and set up a local organization. I saw this as an opportunity for a renewal of practice. The process began with hope. My role was to be an educator and unpaid consultant. I was able to present workshops on topics such as, "what is organizing" and "how to negotiate." I met with citizens from the area and a small group of youth who were being trained to work as local organizers. There was an ongoing process of outreach through knocking on doors to talk about specific conditions such as housing, crime, and traffic. There were actions, sometimes spontaneous. For example, a young single mother, who had just become involved with our group, picketed an intersection with a couple of friends and children, demanding that drivers slow down and respect traffic signs. Gradually, citizens formed themselves into a group, nominated some leaders, and spoke for the neighbourhood. This was a good beginning, a hopeful start. For me, it was fun to watch people who had rarely had a voice come forward and begin to play an active role in shaping their neighbourhood.

However, there were problems at many levels. One was the jealousy of other local organizations who felt they had a mandate to represent the interests of the residents and were uncomfortable about the fact that the residents wanted their own voice. However, there were some crucial errors made in the organizing that led to a replication of some of the worst characteristics of other community groups. As the group evolved, a leader came forward who was both powerful and dynamic and fundamentally anti-democratic. She would not tolerate any criticism and internal debate. There was little place for anyone else except people who passively accepted her role. Further, one of the tactics used by the organization was to invite the mayor during his re-election campaign of 1998 to spend a weekend in the neighbourhood to "see how the other half (more like 85 per cent) lives." The mayor was down in the polls and faced the prospect of a defeat. His visit turned his campaign around as he transformed himself into a populist. He subsequently won. This tactic put the group on the map, and it received a huge boost in its public image and legitimacy, particularly with the city administration. However, rather than using the event as a tactic, the group became more drawn into the political process and became viewed by others in the community as an uncritical ally of the mayor and his party. One of the rewards was to receive funding from a new municipal program. However, the victory further isolated the group from other community organizations.

The group secured a minimum of funding and opened a storefront office. But the tension continued and grew. The grassroots activities diminished, and people spent time in the storefront arguing among themselves and trying to parlay their alliance with the city into more secure funding. Periodically there was outreach and attempts to broaden the organizational base by recruiting interested residents, but the problem was that there was no room for new members within the organization. My role continued through this process. I met with a core group of staff and some of the more active board members one morning every second week. We discussed what should be done, planned campaigns, and examined ways to develop skills that could be used in the organizing process. Yet, nothing happened, and I began to spend more and more time mediating conflicts. The final straw for me was the collaboration of the leader of the organization with a city staff member on a plan to provide funds for community organizations. The process was undemocratic and provoked opposition from many of the groups and community leaders that I had known and worked with in other capacities. I was able to support the opposition by providing a secret, first draft of the program. It became clear that the goal of the leader of the organization and the small group around her was to secure funds regardless of the political costs. I decided at that point to leave the organization.

This experience has provoked reflection about the limits and possibilities of grassroots organizing. Processes at the community level have become highly professional and are cut-off from the traditions of social activism. There is much discussion about social/political/economic determinants, but it is necessary to understand the role of agency in the process, how we each shape practice and use opportunities. It is easy to fall into deterministic assumptions, but practice is never uniform; there are always cracks in the dominant structure and examples of grassroots challenges to those with power.

It is this tension that shapes opportunities for the promotion of opposition and democracy. We as activists and organizers have to learn to recognize, seize, and support these periods to strengthen the movement of social and political opposition. To find these spaces we need to consider the two intertwining factors of agency and context. As an activist, the perspectives and ideologies that I carry with me were shaped in the period of my own political and social awakening. The context has shifted. There are fewer opportunities for social activism; the openings are narrower, but they do exist. The restructuring of the economy and the state should not be read as the beginning of the end for community organization's role in providing opposition to government and the wider system of globalized capitalism. The current period is creating a renewed opposition, outside of community and often led by young activists, who directly confront corporate power on the world stage. The question for me is whether these new activist activities will have an impact on the community sector and shake it up.

Community organizing does not exist in a vacuum, but is stimulated by the social and political movements of each historical period. Movements created for civil rights, women's liberation, peace, and ecology were founded alongside those that provided traditional and innovative services. Some organizations stimulated by these social movements, at least in their early stages, continued to struggle in opposition. They brought democratic processes into the workplace; they challenged professionalism and hierarchies; they continued to battle for social justice, either as advocates or through direct mobilization. Over the years, often because of a weakening of the social movements and an isolation of the community organization or because of the pressures of the demands of their funders, most of these initiatives have lost their radical politics and have become professionally driven service providers.

I have mentioned the tension between community organizations and short-lived social movements and their cadre of politically motivated activists. I question whether or not the activists will find a place within community organizations, what kind of openness there will be for them, and what kind of challenges they will bring. As I have started this book with my experiences, I will continue with the voices of some of these new activists, whom I have interviewed. They bring a strong social commitment to their activities; their politics comes out of older traditions, but, at the same time, they bring a new and different voice. The continuities and discontinuities will shape the dialogue between generations.

CHAPTER TWO

EXPLORING MODELS, THEORY, AND LEARNING FROM HISTORY

Community organizing practice has rich traditions. Although experience in the real world is the motor that drives it, theory and models can be useful as guides. There is a healthy tension between the two, one that is not easily resolved. In this chapter, I will outline theoretical positions and models of practice in order to help understand community organizing and to be more explicit about its underpinnings. This will not be a literature review, but I have selectively drawn on the literature in order to come to grips with practice questions. Three topics will be covered: values and theory, practice models, and the historical development of community organizing, with an emphasis on Quebec.

The difficulty I face with this task is that, by its very nature, community organizing begins with the complexities of practice. Creating processes that can lead to change in peoples' lives is, to say the least, a daunting task. It requires many skills, long hours, perseverance, and, out of necessity, pragmatism. Trade-offs are part of the day-to-day reality. The basic values and theoretical perspectives of the organizers can be lost in the fast-moving realities of development and struggle. Yet, at the same time, existing theories and models, despite the fact that they do not easily connect to the "real world" of social and political engagement, can contribute to our analysis and vision. Furthermore, the forces that shape practice do not come from either texts or the practitioner. More often, they are structured by wider political and economic conditions, which, in turn, can shape the availability of support for community organizations. In other words, employees of community organizations have to play the game of finding support for their activities within existing boundaries and structures. This process has a major impact on practice by forcing those in the field to believe that pragmatism and compromise can be their only guiding values. At best, there are tensions between these forces that shape initiatives in the field and the ideas that guide them. At worst, there is little reflection on practice, and it is defined in relation to specific social objectives and limited by resources available to carry out a program of activities. I believe that, without critical reflection, there is profound political danger. We are doomed to fall into patterns defined by those with resources, and, in the process, we lose our vision of what we were trying to do in the first place. Therefore, this chapter will try to make explicit those aspects that are often lost in the day-to-day—the complex interconnections between values and theory, practice models, and the historical development of community organizing—in hopes of contributing to the shaping of vision and strategy for community organizers in the future.

I face a particular tension in bridging the worlds of practice and the university. My role as teacher and researcher pushes me toward trying to find perspectives that can contribute toward both an understanding and an analysis of practice. In order to teach it, I am required to discern patterns of practice and present theory that helps students to analyze it. At the same time, I am driven not only by my own involvement in the field but by the demands of students to bring the discussion down to earth and to face the question of how theory and models contribute to the everyday demands of practice. The challenge to balance the two is one that is enriching and difficult.

There are fundamental issues that go beyond either the immediacy of practice or an academic stance towards it. I keep returning to the nagging question at the core: what does community organizing contribute to the process of social change? This is not an academic question, but it is the issue on which all the other questions turn, the issue that haunts those of us on the left, who have looked to community organizing as one vehicle to promote social justice, reshape power relations, challenge the privilege of the few, and create a voice for the powerless. Fundamentally, I ask that community organizing contribute to the process of opposition in our society, by resisting capitalism, patriarchy, racism, and environmental destruction. This process needs to be grounded in day-to-day struggles, while, at the same time, it promotes a wider vision and analysis. The interaction of pragmatism and vision is complex, but both are necessary. Without the former, there will be no participation of citizens in action; without the latter, we are condemned to be travelling without maps, never knowing where we will end up. In this chapter, I will keep in mind the tension between visions of social change and pragmatic engagements in the field. Historical material and examples will be provided as a place to begin looking at the models, theories, and underlying values of community organizing. Finally comes the question of how to understand the connections between these traditions, values, and models and the underlying issue of social change.

DEFINITIONS

Providing a definition of community organizing is a necessary first step. Rubin and Rubin (1992) provide a useful starting point. They argue:

> Community organizing is a search for social power and an effort to combat perceived helplessness through learning that what appears personal is often political.... Community organizing creates a capacity for democracy and for sustained social change. It can make society more adaptable and governments more accountable.... Community organizing means bringing people together to combat shared problems and to increase their say about decisions that affect their lives. (pp. 1, 3)

Several elements are important in this statement. The first is "social power," which stands in contrast to "perceived helplessness." Social power is gained through collective action, the core of organizing. We will see how power is used in different ways. One tradition—community action—sees power as a way to push others to do something about group needs such as housing or neighbourhood improvements. The other—personal development—is the power to help oneself through collective action. This can include building local institutions to provide social or economic betterment. Second is learning. Rubin and Rubin focus on the movement from the personal to the political. Learning, which is a participatory process that teaches about how power operates and what can be done to advance one's interests, is essential in all processes of organizing. Through these processes, individuals can develop many skills and learn to become leaders. Thus, processes in community organizing contribute to both personal and social change.

"Capacity for democracy" is the third key element. Democracy has to be understood in the widest sense possible as the process by which people gain control of aspects of their own lives through organizations in which they have a voice. This is in contrast to the dominant notion of democracy, which is periodic voting and participation in the electoral process (see Chapter 3 for a discussion of the emergence of direct and participatory democracy with community and social organizations). Through community organizing, people can learn to shape decisions in organizations that touch their lives and to exert pressure to create responsiveness from different levels of government. Democratic practice at the local level, as both an outcome and an ongoing process, is one of the most important contributions of community organizing. However, one central question is the breadth of its influence. There are many local success stories: citizens have created democratic organizations, enlarged opportunities for participation, and have been able to influence decision-making. However, whether these events have created a more democratic society is problematic. Strong central authorities in our society, controlled either by business interests or their allies in traditional political parties, provide few opportunities for democratic accountability to the wider population. Moving from the local to the state or to corporate power is the core challenge: what are the limits of organizing in shaping democratic processes in the wider society? Finally, Rubin and Rubin (1992) introduce "sustained social change" as an outcome. This, perhaps, is the most difficult aspect of their definition. They suggest five goals of social change: improvement of the quality of life through the resolution of shared problems; reduction of the level of social inequalities caused by poverty, racism, and sexism; the exercise and preservation of democratic values as part of the process of organizing; enabling people to achieve their potential as individuals; and the creation of a sense of community (p. 10). The difficulty with this list is the mixture of goals that can be realized locally and those that require state intervention, changes in social policy, or changes in the wider economy and society. Issues like inequality cannot be improved at the local level, although they affect communities directly, but groups from the local level can be involved in wider campaigns to pressure for such changes. Before turning to a discussion of theory and values, a discussion of the history of community organizing with two case examples will illustrate the realities—and the limits—of practice.

HISTORICAL PERSPECTIVES

Throughout history, people have joined together for mutual aid or to demand social justice. However, we will concentrate on the ideas, strategies, and changes in community organization that have taken place over the last 40 years. Although I draw on examples from Quebec, because it is the place where I have been most directly involved, the experience there is not unique. For example, Hasson and Ley (1994) in their case studies of neighbourhood organizing in Vancouver and Jerusalem argue that organizing has gone through several stages. The urban protest movements of the 1960s and 1970s displaced the paternalism associated with political machines and/or charity. The period that followed was characterized by partnership or co-production between community and government. Fisher (1994) identifies similar stages in the United States. Using this idea of stages, I will divide the history into three periods that reflect wider socio-political shifts and related changes in practice. There are continuities and overlaps in practices between the periods, but differences in the type of practice that prevailed in different times. Two cases illustrate these continuities and differences. The first, from the late 1960s and early 1970s, is an example of an action, the mobilization approach typical of that period. The second, from the 1980s, describes a service based on the community development approach. Chapters 3 and 4 will explore the traditions raised by these examples in more depth.

1. THE 1960S AND 1970S: "IN YOUR FACE": CONFRONTING POWER

The 1960s and 1970s were a time of renewal for community organizing. The spirit of social optimism made basic change seem possible. Many community organizations existed prior to the period; however, they were linked to social services and charity provided by religious or cultural groups for their members. The new departure in the community sector was the creation of organizations able to mobilize people to help them find a voice on a variety of social issues and to challenge the dominant social order (see Doucet and Favreau, 1991; Favreau, 1989; Panet-Raymond and Mayer, 1997). At the same time, the federal and provincial governments enlarged the welfare state and provided funds to support social innovation through grants either to encourage employment for the young (Opportunities for Youth) or to create short-term jobs during periods of high unemployment (Local Initiative Programs) (Keck and Fulks, 1997). Other funding, available from many government departments, supported new approaches in the social and health services. One of the main characteristics of the community movement was its autonomy, which was not directly undermined by such funding, and, in some cases, its withdrawal provoked angry confrontations. Whether new services were established or protests and pressure groups were formed, the separation of the groups from the state was strongly guarded, and the structure of organizations and their vision and activities were not directly shaped by funding.

The Greater Montreal Anti-Poverty Coordinating Committee (GMAPCC)[1] is an example of direct action organizing. It was founded in the spring of 1970 by a coalition of local English-speaking citizens' groups, representing five welfare rights committees composed mainly of welfare recipients, along with two-full time organizers (Benello, 1972). GMAPCC's initial mandate was to organize the community around welfare rights and advocacy:

> (GMAPCC taught) people the power of group participation through successful actions against the welfare office. It [created] a strong body of informed welfare recipients who [were] in a position to demand changes from the government over the laws which concerned their lives. (PERM, 1971)

By 1972, GMAPCC had adopted a statement of principles that covered a broad range of topics: jobs and income, housing and urban renewal, education, justice, consumer protection, mass media, democracy, women, racism, the elderly, workers and unions, language and nationalism, and big business (GMAPCC, 1972). These positions advocated redistribution of income and wealth through strong government action.

GMAPCC's mandate was carried out in a number of ways. First, confrontational tactics were aimed at winnable objectives:

> GMAPCC and the groups relating to it have focussed heavily on conflict situations and on high visibility confrontations, where pressure is brought to bear on the government at various levels. It creates a clear enemy, and focuses discontent; the motive power is rage and the structural aspect of Oppression is minimised in

---

[1] The information in this section is based in part on an article written by Anna Kruzynski and Eric Shragge (1999). Documents consulted were gathered through a community/popular archives project in Pointe St-Charles in Montreal, and interviews with activists were conducted by students during the years 1993 to 1999 as assignments in courses in the School of Social Work at McGill University.

favour of personifying the enemy—a mayor, a corporation president, a slumlord. (Benello, 1972, p. 476)

These disruptive tactics included occupations, sit-ins, and demonstrations at welfare offices and other institutions (Shragge, 1994). Second, individual advocacy was used to ensure that individuals' rights were protected from the abusive ways of the welfare institution. Advocates—citizens who were trained in the rules of the law—accompanied welfare recipients to the welfare office to plead for social assistance. Thus, one of the main roles of the resource people within GMAPCC was to seek out, politicize, and train local leadership. This was accomplished in a variety of ways. "Kitchen meetings" brought interested citizens from a particular neighbourhood together with the resource people to discuss issues of concern to poor people in their area. The goal of these meetings was to get citizens to participate in GMAPCC actions and to eventually form their own local citizens' group. Second, regular workshops for local organizers, for members present at general meetings, and for member groups at their request were developed to give participants the tools with which to organize and build groups; topics included the "dos and don'ts" of organizing, negotiating, block organizing, public relations with the press, tactics, and power structures.

The first action that GMAPCC organized, in July 1970, centred on the right to have an advocate present when requesting social assistance. Their spokesman explained why the group was demonstrating:

> Many people have a hard time speaking for themselves when they apply for welfare—they're too intimidated....
> Our members have studied the rules and they can help an applicant as well or better than any lawyer. (Cited in Radwanski, 1970)

A succession of successful actions followed. For example, the "needy-mother sit-in" resulted in the granting of all their demands: "decentralization of welfare operations, parity rates for all welfare recipients, and availability of immediate assistance for emergency cases"

(Arnopoulos, 1970). In January 1971, GMAPCC staged a successful demonstration in front of a slumlords house, demanding adequate repairs and restoration of heat in apartments of citizens of Pointe St. Charles (PERM, 1971). In one action, 22 people were arrested at a sit-in against the poor treatment of women, racism, and late cheques at the Atwater welfare office. GMAPCC was quick to follow this with one of its largest actions, the "St-Denis sit-in," which initiated a number of meetings with Minister of Social Affairs Claude Castonguay (Benello, 1972). A series of publications entitled "Welfare means hunger and slavery" was produced for this action, providing rationale and evidence of feasibility for the demands for increases to welfare rates, removal of the policy that limited the benefits of single "employable" young adults, and installation of hospitality booths in all welfare offices. Once again, GMAPCC managed to win its demands:

> Claude Castonguay told a group of anti-poverty workers that ... a general increase in the [welfare] payments is expected ... starting in the fall, a few offices will begin issuing welfare cheques every 14 days to make budgeting easier for the recipients.... He also agreed with the groups' demands for hospitality booths in Montreal welfare offices because they had proven to be useful in provincial offices. (Ferrante, 1972)

Finally, in 1973, GMAPCC launched a successful campaign to stop Bell Canada's proposal to increase pay-phone rates from 10 to 25 cents.

GMAPCC enjoyed many victories for welfare rights and had a significant impact on the people who participated in its development. Not only did they have a direct effect on government policy and practice, but welfare recipients had become citizens. This lesson is important. The poor were not "given" rights; they claimed them. Organizations like GMAPCC argued that reform from above was not acceptable unless the poor and others affected by change were to have a voice, that effective representation implied active engagement of the poor people themselves. GMAPCC was not solely responsible for the gains made in that period, but it was part of a wider social movement that was pushing for social change at a time of economic expansion and social reform.

Other services were not primarily concerned with direct action, but were organized by both outside activists and local residents. They embodied similar values and orientations and supported the efforts of social activists. For example, clinics, such as the one established in 1968 in the working-class neighbourhood of Pointe St. Charles (Shragge, 1990), pioneered a new approach to health care. It is important to remember that when the clinic was established, there was no public health insurance; patients paid doctors directly and privately. If an individual could not afford to pay, she/he either did not seek medical services or used charity clinics. In other words, health care was not a right.

The Pointe St. Charles clinic was established by a coalition of medical students and young doctors and nurses who were influenced by the radical politics of the period, along with community organizers and local residents. They had a wider vision of health care than the traditional medical illness model. They believed that ill health was connected to poverty and its related housing, working, and general living conditions. As a result, their practice incorporated a number of strategies, ranging from direct medical consultation to a variety of collective actions, often in alliance with other local organizations. The issue of health care moved from the diagnosis and treatment of individual illness to a social analysis that saw social change as the cure. In addition, the clinic challenged the monopoly of professionals over the definition and delivery of health care. Residents of the community were trained as community health workers, and an active democratic process resulted in professional accountability, not domination. The clinic still exists. It has grown in size and provides similar services to those provided by the network of government community clinics across the province. However, unlike the others, it is not a government agency, but a community organization, with an assembly of local residents as the supreme decision-making body. Although it has become more bureaucratic with its growth and large mandate, it still has been able to support and lead a variety of community action projects and social struggles.

I have included this example to demonstrate that service provision, the "social work" model discussed by Fisher (1994), is not necessarily limited to services, but can maintain a social change agenda. These two directions—social action and service—continue in the community movement, one demanding changes in policy from the government, either as an advocate for different social groups or through the mobilization of those groups themselves, while the other builds local organizations that provide a range of democratically controlled health and social services.

The spirit of the 1960s and 1970s provided an opening for social experimentation. A stable and growing economy and a corresponding strengthening and expansion of the trade union movement shaped the possibilities. The challenges issued by both the trade unions and the community went beyond the ideologies of capitalism and promoted fundamental change based on a socialist vision. Further, community organizations, with their demands for a democratization of social institutions, created for many participants an experience of direct democracy that demonstrated the capacity of people to manage their own lives and institutions. These traditions will be explored in more detail in the chapter that follows.

2. THE 1980S: WHOSE COMMUNITY? PROFESSIONALIZATION AND COMMUNITY SERVICE

The 1980s was a period of transition between the tough-minded politicization of the previous decades and the redefined role of the community sector within the global capitalism of the 1990s. In order to understand this transition, we can look at shifts in both state policy and in the community movement itself. In response to changes in the economy with the end of a long period of economic growth and stability, new solutions were sought by political leaders. Conservative Prime Minister Margaret Thatcher in Britain and Republican President Ronald Reagan in the United States inaugurated a new era dominated by neo-conservative beliefs and policies. Spending on developing the welfare state and in general was cut, the power of workers was attacked, and unemployment was allowed to rise. The community movement and the trade unions responded to these changes with uncertainty and a defensive posture.

At the same time, identity politics and social movements reshaped the community sector. Following the lead of the women's movement, groups such as gays and lesbians, the disabled, immigrants, and people who had survived the psychiatric system created new services and programs that they could shape and control. Examples include rape crisis centres and shelters to combat violence against women. Similarly, services for the disabled not only were places of social provision but also helped reshape the way these groups were viewed and treated in the wider society. The emphasis was on social rights and the building of new opportunities. Two directions were manifested: demands for political recognition and legitimacy from government and the establishment of alternative services that combined participatory practices and new and innovative approaches to service (Lustiger-Thaler and Shragge, 1993).

The rapid expansion of the community sector, with its shift from mobilization and political education to service, required skilled providers with university training or on-the-job experience, thus encouraging a growing sophistication and professionalism. A new relationship between the community movement and the state, particularly at the provincial level, began (Hamel and Léonard, 1980; Panet-Raymond, 1987). Many community initiatives, begun as experimental models, became adjuncts to state services as a result of the decentralization of government services and the clear fiscal limits of state support. In Quebec, funding came from the provincial government, and negotiations took place through "regroupements" or sectoral coalitions of, for example, representatives from rape crisis centres, alternative mental health agencies, and neighbourhood groups. The politics and policies of service were played out through these relations. This does not imply that the activism, mobilization, and direct action associated with the earlier period disappeared, but that these activities and engagements declined relative to the new directions (Panet-Raymond and Mayer, 1997). Divisions deepened between those community organizations that defined their services in an alternative perspective and those that emphasized professional-ism and traditional organizational structures (White 1997). The funding from government, the service delivery agenda, and the expansion of the responsibilities of community organizations decreased their involvement in political and social struggles. Thus, in the context of an economic downturn and a reduction in support for the welfare state, the size of the community sector grew. The emphasis was on service provision, often innovative, with increased professionalism and a more formalized relationship with the state. As a consequence, community organizations lessened their participation in the mobilization of their respective constituencies, substituting representation by professionals. At best, advocacy replaced direct action organizing, often within the framework of the promotion of services rather than raising demands for social change. Community organizing was reshaped from a process of grassroots development and conflicts to innovative and professionalized services representing the needs and "interests" of their clients.

The economic and policy directions that began in the early 1980s intensified with increased unemployment and the disappearance of industrial jobs in older working-class neighbourhoods. As a result, urban poverty grew. Along with the economic decline, all levels of government maintained cost-cutting measures, mostly aimed at social programs. Yet, building on the capacity and the organization of the community sector, more stable relationships were established between them and the government. The tendency of the previous period to give both responsibility and some forms of assistance to community services continued and were consolidated and formalized through structured partnerships (Panet-Raymond, 1992). Service delivery with prescribed norms, defined by particular program-related funds, began to shape the community-state relation. Conflicts were played out in the process of negotiation between regional bodies that allocated funds and the various sectoral organizations that brought together community-based services. At the same time, oppo-sition was still expressed by some groups who continued to work politically through coalitions, particularly those opposing major changes in unemployment benefits or social aid. However, these coalitions had little success in either reversing government policy or in mobilizing large numbers of people affected by policy changes.

Beginning in the mid-1980s, new initiatives, such as the formation of Community Economic Development (CED) organizations, were pursued by the community sector as a means to counter economic deterioration (Fontan, 1988, 1994). Government agencies from the municipal to the federal level coordinated their allocation of funds and shaped the activities of these agencies. Some of these groups used government workfare programs to organize ways in which those excluded from the job market could find training, while, at the same time, they built local networks of social solidarity (Shragge and Deniger, 1997). Others linked practices to train individuals to participate in the labour market with socially oriented community businesses (Ninacs, 1997). These new practices created a space for those marginalized by the economic crisis and a way of building cultural and social alternatives, which represented the beginnings of a small social economy among the poor. Yet, at the same time, the process transformed these organizations into managers of government programs and promoters of local, private economic (capitalist) development (Fontan and Shragge, 1998). This tension became clear in the case of Chic Resto-Pop.[2]

Twelve welfare recipients organized a community restaurant, Resto-Pop, in 1984. They had two purposes: to create jobs for the founding members and others on social assistance and to provide nutritious, hot, and inexpensive meals for the poor in the community. When these goals were realized, the organization began to expand in size and to broaden its activities. It introduced a mobile kitchen to provide meals to local schools and instituted summer day camps for area school children. In addition, a musical festival (which is now part of an autonomous organization) was introduced in 1992. Resto-Pop served three meals a day, five days a week. In 1984, it served meals for 50 people, in 1990 for 250, and by 1995 it reached 800 customers.

Resto-Pop was set up as a non-profit organization managed by a seven-member Board of Directors, who came from organizations of

---

[2] This material on Chic Resto-Pop is based on an article by Fontan and Shragge (1996).

the Catholic church and the professions, such as psychologists, and were almost equally divided between men and women. There was no staff representative on the board, and initially there was no general assembly. The operating budget for 1994 was $800,000. Slightly less than half came from the three levels of government; the rest was raised from sales of meals, bingo, and donations. In 1998, there were 19 full-time employees under the supervision of the director. Four employees were involved with administrative work, two co-coordinated the restaurant, and 15 others carried out the general work.

Resto-Pop self-study reports showed that their most frequent customers were single men, with an average age of 45, who lived alone, and received welfare or Employment Insurance. On average, they ate six to eight meals a week there. Resto-Pop not only provided meals, it also became a place for socializing with others in a similar situation. The large dining room was also used by community organizations for the provision of information and discussion of such issues as the social origins of poverty and the rights of those receiving welfare. Thus, Resto-Pop was simultaneously a training program, a socially supportive environment for the poor in the community, and a restaurant servicing its community.

To carry out its mandate for job development and training, Resto-Pop brought in 105 trainees a year on an ongoing basis. The length of training varied between six and 15 months, and all the trainees were welfare recipients and participants in one of the workfare programs called Expérience de travail (EXTRA), which limited the period of time in which training could be funded. This program was a controversial part of a welfare reform introduced in 1988, and many community organizations that could accept trainees boycotted it because it did not create real jobs, and the lack of jobs made whatever training was received useless. Resto-Pop members believed that the program was in the interest of welfare recipients, as a means of connecting those marginalized by poverty to a wider social process in which their labour was the basis of social reintegration:

> Quebec is not only confronted with a crisis of jobs,
> but also by a transformation in work. Faced with this

> transformation, one must not only reaffirm the princi-
> ple of citizenship, one must also guarantee a minimal
> income to citizens, recognizing the existence and the
> importance of a new type of socially useful work.
> Resto-Pop works in this direction. (translation, ES)

Thus, Resto-Pop attempted to use the shifting economy and the redefined welfare state as a way to become part of a wider movement in Quebec to create a locally based social economy.

According to one staff member, who supervised the trainees, participants were treated as workers with the responsibilities and rights attached to that role, in an attempt to break the dependency and passivity associated with individuals who have received Social Aid (welfare) for a long period. The goals of the training were to promote socially useful work that permitted the individual to rebuild confidence, improve general work habits, and learn new job-oriented skills.

The coordinator of Resto-Pop explained that one of the most important functions of the organization was to support the trainees. Psychological support and literacy training were provided by a neighbourhood organization, along with a variety of programs linked to the preparation to work. The content of the training went beyond the immediate tasks necessary to running a community restaurant, including topics such as social rights. The longer term goal of training, according to one of the founders and a former coordinator of Resto-Pop, was to demonstrate that the marginalized people of the district could be other than clients of the services of community organizations—they could also be workers and effective managers.

In the fall of 1995, Resto-Pop moved in a new direction. The staff person in charge of training raised several concerns about the training and related government policies. He argued that the government continued to think about and to apply its welfare system as though it were one of last resort, as if the recipients had invented their own joblessness. Short-term training programs coupled with unemployment had institutionalized instability and excluded many people, especially parents, from meaningful economic and social roles. In light of this analysis, Resto-Pop asked the government to reform its training program to allow participants to work for three years. The government refused, arguing that it did not want to encourage dependence in a protected environment.

Frustrated by the government's lack of movement in a more progressive direction and by the continuing increase in local poverty, the leaders of Resto-Pop called a conference to examine underlying economic issues, the politics of deficit cutting, and the lack of adequate government response. Several hundred community members participated in this event, culminating in a series of demands and a march to the office of their local provincial representative. Their demands touched fiscal and monetary policy, minimum wage, job creation, day care, and training and called for full employment through a variety of actions and innovations (Chic Resto-Pop, 1995). This high-profile and successful event put Resto-Pop on the map as a leader in the debate on poverty in Quebec. It demonstrated how pressure could be put on government and launched a public debate within the new model of practice that has become dominant in the 1990s.

3. THE 1990S AND BEYOND: MOVING AWAY, MOVING TOWARDS

The community practices developed in the 1990s incorporated the formal partnership arrangements discussed above into the structures of their organizations and their wider relationships. Community organizations were faced with the dilemma that greater recognition and funding actually diminished their autonomy and reinforced a service agenda. With this orientation, groups shifted from a membership or social movement base to a client focus. This redefinition is inherently depoliticizing. Clients are to be served and have a less active—or no—role in either the organizations' internal processes or on wider social issues. At best, they are represented rather than mobilized. Thus, the form of political representation became lobbying by coalitions of community organizations promoting the needs of a particular population. For instance, the event organized by Chic Resto-Pop was initiated primarily by the staff and did not follow up with any kind of sustained mobilization or on-going campaign.

Some groups maintained the earlier traditions of mobilization and direct action. For instance, in 1995 the Fédération des femmes du Québec organized a march from Montreal to Quebec City called Bread and Roses. This march of several thousand women called attention to issues of poverty and violence against women. With the success of this event the women participated in the organization of an international event—the World March of Women in the fall of 2000. Supported by the community movement, this event brought 30,000 into the streets of Montreal and equally large numbers in many other places across the globe. Even though the majority of community organizations have become involved in a service or development model, the success of this march demonstrates that these groups and organizations still have sympathy for direct action, although it is no longer the dominant element in their practices.

Clearly, the community movement has changed over the last 40 years. It has moved from an oppositional force to one that is both highly professional and integrated into the state service sector as an important partner; at the same time, traces of the earlier stances and values remain. Is it possible to describe the community sector as contributing to the processes of social change? Deena White (1997) summarizes its changes as follows:

> The Quebec government, through its efforts to integrate community-level collective action into its social policies, has made considerable headway in transforming radical politics into interest-group politics, grassroots unrest into services by and for vulnerable social groups, and confrontation into apparent consensus. (p. 81)

This argument can lead to pessimistic conclusions. Other analysts see more positive possibilities. Panet-Raymond and Mayer (1997) argue that community groups have used a strategy of "critical cooperation or cooperative conflict" (p. 51) in their relationship with the state and that both radical advocacy groups with their coalitions and institutionalized service organizations co-exist in tension. Thus, community organizations are pulled between two poles. The first pole is to work in opposition by raising demands, mobilizing or representing the needs of their constituency, and pushing for some form of social change. The second, and more common practice, is to become extensions of the state; by receiving government funding, organizations become partners with the state in the provision of services. It is this change that leads me to question the role of the community sector as a vehicle for social justice.

The current conjuncture presents limits, problems, and possibilities. With changes in the economy and the state's withdrawal or reduction of its commitments to social provision, the community sector has begun to play an enlarged social role. It has taken over responsibilities for various services and entered the chambers of state to be consulted on policy issues. These might be seen as gains and opportunities; however, the consequence has been that the community movement may have lost its critical edge and radical democratic practice. Some argue that the new relationship with the state is "cooperative conflict" (Panet-Raymond and Mayer, 1997, p. 51), but questions remain. What is the source of power that can sustain a conflictual relation with any credibility? What is the power base of community organizations if they cannot mobilize people? How can they defend their autonomy without an active politicized constituency? What happens if the only source of legitimacy is the capacity of the community sector to provide inexpensive and innovative services and to administer programs?

The answers to these questions are contingent upon a professionalized leadership in community organizations. From the beginning many different professionals, both those with university training and those with on-the-job experience, have been involved with groups and organizations. The problem arises when expertise becomes a barrier to the participation of citizens. Organizations require staff who can provide services. The tasks and work of the community sector are far too complex and the work too time-consuming for voluntarism. One consequence is the power of professional expertise to take control away from the wider community of the organization. This process contributes to demobilization and gradually results in passivity in which people become transformed into "clients" rather than citizens (McKnight, 1995B). Equally, there is a danger that the work of the community sector will come to rest on the shoulders of volunteers, who may not have the requisite training or experience to deal with day-to-day activities, much less the continuing evolution of the organizations. A constructive tension is needed between an active membership participation and a staff accountable to the organization.

The service orientation itself has contributed to a demobilization of citizens. Within this orientation there are a wide variety of practice and forms, ranging from self-help groups like collective kitchens, to new community businesses specializing in training, to services for different populations. Many forms of management co-exist, everything from collectives to traditional hierarchical forms. Yet, the common purpose is social provision. The tradition of community organizations as a voice of opposition has shifted. Fewer and fewer groups directly organize and mobilize the poor and the disadvantaged. Rather, those groups still involved in oppositional activities represent populations affected by changes in government policies, sometimes defining their self-interest as service providers as the cause to be defended. Service provision and mobilization are not necessarily in contradiction, but, as an organization becomes enmeshed in the demands of provision and as governments support only the service aspects of their programs, integrating other activities becomes more difficult. Further, the community sector is not well-financed, and, for most organizations, there are no long-term guarantees. A relationship of dependency with little equality is thus established, leading to less risk-taking and political engagement.

There are some organizations still engaged in the older traditions of mobilization and organization of citizens at the local level as a means of opposition. The World March of Women in 2000 is a good example, as is the rapid growth of anti-corporate social activism in recent years, such as the demonstrations in Seattle against the World Trade Organization (WTO) at the end of 1999 and the campaign against the Multi-Lateral Agreement on Investment (MAI) that, at least temporarily, blocked that agreement. As discussed in the previous chapter and as we shall see in Chapter 5, the relationship between these social movements and community organizations is not well-defined. Their opposition to globalization is supported by mass mobilization, putting people in the streets. In the community sector, the opposition comes from coalitions of organizations, or "Tables de Concertation," which is a form of representation of interest rather than a mobilization of people to represent themselves. The strength of the community movement, going back to the late 1960s, was found in its capacity to mobilize people into action, either to protest and confront governments or to build new forms of local democracy. The danger of the current conjuncture is that a professionalized, service-oriented community sector will be legitimized by its competency to serve and represent. At the same time it will lose, if it hasn't already, its real source of power—that is, organized and active citizens, struggling on their own behalf. With these examples and transitions in mind, we will now generalize the discussion by examining values, theory, and models of practice.

VALUES AND THEORY

In my teaching and practice, I find there is a dichotomy that I, as well as others engaged in community organizing, confront. On the one hand, we have constructed a strong critical analysis of the inequalities of class, gender, and race that are inherent in the social, political, and economic system; for many of us, this includes a critique of the impact of the economy from an ecological perspective. On the other hand, our practices are shaped by the need for pragmatic and concrete results. As a consequence, practice seems to be shaped by theories derived from moderate frameworks and conventional assumptions. The radical analysis leads one to conclude that society needs to be transformed, while the practice, at best, brings about small incremental reforms. So, how do we combine a critical analysis with our practice? This is a difficult task, and one that evades simplistic solutions. The question, however, needs to be confronted, even if the responses are partial.

In order to explore these issues, we need theory. Theoretical discussions are assumed to be abstract, distant from reality, boring, and
an unnatural pursuit of academics with too much time on their
hands. However, theory needs to be understood as "[an] attempt to
make sense of ... encounters with the world, to look for patterns and
regularities in order to predict the outcomes of ... actions ... the
overall purpose being to create greater understanding of the world"
(Popple, 1995, p. 31). In their proposal for the construction of a "liberating theory," Albert et al. (1986) acknowledge the tensions in the
use of social theory. They state:

> social theories cannot help us make testable predic-
> tions in the manner of physics and chemistry.... But,
> nonetheless, we can use powerful social theory to
> explain relationships; to envision possibilities and
> delineate trends that may impede or promote those
> possibilities; and to make "probabilistic predictions"
> about likely outcomes of current activities. (p. 5)

Our expectations of theory, therefore, have to be limited; it can be
used as a guide rather than a recipe for social change. But theory
does not necessarily reside solely in the minds of those who write
books. Lemert (1993) reminds us that the construction of theory is
an everyday practice used in order to understand social and power
relations. He cites the example of his son, who upon transferring
from an alternative school to a traditional one and observing the differences in culture, particularly the discipline of queuing in sex-seg-
regated lines before class, theorized that education was really about
social control and discipline. Community organization can both
draw from traditional theories and engage in a process of "commonsense" theorizing, which allows us to understand the processes
around us and how social intervention can bring about social change.
This raises two overlapping premises. The first comes from a perspective shaped by examining our underlying values and constructing
a basic social standpoint. It tries to set out both an analysis of the
society and, at times, a prescriptive outlook and vision with related

goals for social transition. The second, which often accompanies the first, is a theory about how change takes place, including a discussion of human agency and related social processes. Thus, we have two inter-related components—one that helps us shape our social and political vision, and the other that contributes to our understanding of how to achieve these visions.

In order to build a vision of the long-term direction of organizing, acknowledging underlying values is the first step. Fisher (1994) uses four perspectives that shape our stance and help us to name the objectives that we are working towards. He calls the first a reactionary perspective, shaped by values that promote efforts to stop social change and to decrease the power of the lower class and minority groups. The second are those conservative values that attempt to maintain the political and social status quo. It is important to keep these two perspectives in the discussion because there is an illusion that organizing is about promoting social justice and progressive social change. Those on the right have also used organizing techniques to promote their own agendas such as opposition to abortion or gun control. Thus, the introduction of "reactionary" and "conservative" into the discussion is an important reminder that the methods of community organizing can and have been used by the right to defend their interests or to roll back social gains. On the progressive side of the equation, Fisher uses the term "liberal" to describe those who promote more limited social changes that do not actively challenge the existing social and economic system. He uses "radical" to describe those who see the capitalist system as the cause of social problems and organizing as a way to make more basic changes as well as winning concrete gains. Fisher's summary of these political orientations helps us to define our general stance, but they do not illuminate the social and political processes that may lead to social change. They are important, however, because they define basic social visions.

If the aims of community organizing are to win limited reforms, then the liberal perspective is the one that shapes the vision. It prioritizes specific outcomes and focusses strategies on making those gains that bring benefits to the community, such as improved housing conditions or services. Pluralist theory underlies this viewpoint, and it is perhaps the dominant one in community organizing. It argues that power in society is not concentrated in a particular group but is diffused between competing interests. Thus, there is continual bargaining between groups on a variety of social issues and concerns. The state stands outside of these conflicts and plays a role in mediating and resolving disputes and claims from different interest groups. With this perspective, community organizing plays a role "that is acting in supporting and encouraging participation in political and administrative processes" (Popple, 1995, p. 33). Pluralism directs practice to the formation of pressure groups and advocacy for specific social change within the limits of the system.

Fisher's use of the term radical comes from the tradition of the left. The traditional left sought reform either through social democratic parties and the electoral process or through revolution—seizing state power. In both cases the working class was the agent of change, acting through unions and political parties. Community organizing has been problematic because the connections between community and class are unclear. A traditional left critique began with class power and interests and examined the ways that this power operated in the community and how the class struggle could be pursued from the community and in alliance with other working-class organizations. Further, the analysis of the role of the state argued that the state represented the interests of the "ruling class," but with contradictions and tensions that permitted social reforms that played a stabilizing role. Within the community movement, a revolutionary socialist vision was adopted by some organizers particularly in the late 1970s and early 1980s. Popple argues that community workers used this analysis to understand the basic inequalities of capitalism and to pursue class struggle at both a local and regional level, outside of the workplace. The practices in the community itself stayed within the boundaries of pressure group politics as local groups pressured for limited gains that were possible to achieve.

Combining a pragmatic practice with a vision of wider social change and a related strategy is the key to moving community organizing from a liberal to a radical perspective. Immediate goals become subordinated to the democratic processes and politicizing experiences that come with engagement in social struggles. Thus, if a campaign for better housing exposes participants to the structures of wealth and power, discusses collective options such as cooperatives as alternatives, demands state support, and exposes the limits and inherent problems of a market-based housing strategy, then people may become more politicized through that process. In other words, organizing is an opportunity for political education. Further, creating social solidarity and opportunities for participation produces a network of citizens that can act in their collective interest on other questions and join in campaigns on wider issues. Thus, even though the concrete outcomes of a campaign from a pluralist or radical orientation may be the same, the goals of the latter are longer term and linked to an understanding that for fundamental social change to occur ongoing social processes are a necessary precondition.

The feminist movement has made a significant contribution to shaping the vision and processes of community organizing that goes beyond the limits of class analysis. Popple (1995) argues that feminist currents in community work grew out of two perspectives. The first was a critique of the leadership role taken by men in the field of organizing, particularly in the 1960s. The second was a recognition that women and their children represent a key constituency for community workers, and many of the issues and concerns that shaped social struggles flowed from the experiences of women. Therefore, the starting point had to include the experience of women's oppression. Women, who participated in the growing feminist movement of the 1970s, pointed out the theoretical weaknesses in the traditional left theories. They argued that the struggles of women needed to be included as a central element in community organizing. For example, in the United States and Canada, the struggles of welfare mothers for social and economic rights is a vivid example of the process of women taking leadership in a social struggle. At the same time, there were many tensions with male organizers (Kruzynski and Shragge, 1999).

The feminist perspective modified strategies and visions in shaping a wider understanding of what constitutes the struggle for social justice. It is a comprehensive approach to social change. This position is argued by Adamson et al. (1988):

Collective action can reshape our lives and the world around us; it can also change the way we see ourselves—not as individuals struggling in isolation to survive, but as part of a collective of shared interest and vision. This can be a transformative and empowering experience and demonstrates in practice the limits of individualism. Changing society is a way of changing ourselves. (p.155)

This vision of social equality and the connection between personal and political transformation is what forced many organizers to rethink their own values and theories of social change.

Callahan (1997) argues that feminist community development includes all of its traditional elements, but:

what distinguishes feminist community organizing from other approaches is its insistence that all activities must be informed by an analysis of gender (and race and class) and modified on the basis of this analysis. It is also characterized by its commitment to a social movement and by its attempts to connect local efforts to those taking place in other jurisdictions and at other levels. (p. 183)

The links to a wider movement is a crucial point; herein lies one key connection to social change. The danger of any community organizing process is isolation at the local level. Building wider connections to movements for social change is a way to support both a change agenda and this connection between local and wider activism.

Popple discusses anti-racist analysis and practice as another dimension that has important implications for practice. In the United States, the civil rights movement was an impetus for community organizing and social change in Black and other minority communities. The movement had a huge impact on consciousness and energized many different innovations and challenges to the White power structure. In addition, riots and overt rebellion in the cities created conditions that pressured governments there into supporting new social programs that were largely controlled and organized by the Black community and their organizers (Fisher 1994). In Canada and the United Kingdom, anti-racist practice reflects changes in immigration and the growth of new ethnic communities. Resistance to racism had to be integrated into practice, and community work had to provide opportunities for different groups to develop their own cultural formation and build autonomous organizations (Popple 1995). At the same time, these groups challenged the role of White male organizers and their position in many organizations. They pushed the debate further and forced a re-evaluation of the complexities of power. A class-based analysis was not able to get at other forms of oppression, which had to be explicitly acknowledged in order for the struggles against them to be legitimated. Further, new and diverse voices emerged and challenged the wider community movement and sought support from it. Like other aspects of organizing, both feminism and anti-racist perspectives contain elements in common with the radical perspective and acknowledge the necessity of fundamental social change. At the same time, there are tendencies within these perspectives that share a pluralist theoretical framework that favours increasing participation within the system through pressure group activity, rather than challenging its legitimacy.

Gutierrez and Lewis (1995) integrate feminist and anti-racist perspectives. They argue that the goal of organizing is "the elimination of permanent power hierarchies between all people that can prevent them from realizing their human potential. The goal of feminist organizing is the elimination of sexism, racism, and other forms of oppression through the process of empowerment." They see organizing as holistic, bridging differences between women based on such factors as "race, class, physical ability, and sexual orientation with the guiding principle that diversity is strength" (p. 98). One of the most important elements that comes out of feminist and anti-racist writing is the necessity of shifting leadership roles in the organization and thus changing the face of both organizers and leaders. Further, a lens that views the analysis of problems from the perspectives of women and minorities is necessary if power in community organizations is really to shift. Thus, these perspectives integrate connections between race, class, and gender with a process of social inclusion within the organizing process and thus aim at basic social change.

All of these perspectives can be described within the general category of conflict theories. Pluralism examines conflicting group processes, while Marxism, feminism, and anti-racism present an analysis of how power operates in society from the perspectives of class, gender, and race. Clearly, these accounts push community organizing into a conflict mode, challenging the dominant power structure. These are the implicit assumptions of the community action perspective that follows. However, not all approaches to practice share a conflict perspective. The locality or community development model discussed below is shaped by consensus-building, which acts to obscure interest and power. There are a variety of social theories that underpin this approach, including general systems theory that presupposes that all groups in society share common interests and values. The practice that follows leads to support for the dominant power relations and to the creation of community processes that may bring limited improvements to local conditions but not wider social change. As I shall argue, community organizing can be used as a tool to attempt to change society or it can play a far more limited role by changing communities to adapt to the oppression and the dominant interests in society. Thus, we need to acknowledge theories that shape the latter and dispel the illusion that community organizing is automatically connected to a tradition of radical social change.

By outlining these perspectives, are we any further ahead? The basic paradox of using a radical perspective to organize comes in the difference between how we analyze society, how we work towards social change and, related to the latter, how we define and understand social change. The perspectives above are important for making values and analysis explicit. But with the exception of the pluralist and the Marxist perspective, they do not shed much light on the basic question: what are the processes that can bring about progressive social change? This is an extraordinarily difficult question, particularly if one is grounded in the realities of everyday practice. How does one work from a radical stance in organizing and achieve something beyond practice shaped by a pluralist, pressure group orientation? For example, there is often confusion between the militant tactics that a group might use and that would imply a radical stance and their underlying aims of immediate reform or social inclusion. To accomplish a particular goal such as improving local housing conditions, a group might occupy the offices of a municipal housing inspector as a means of getting inspectors to force landlords to make change. However, the practice is still within the limits of the pluralist assumptions about power. Is community organizing limited by the traditions of creating pressure groups, making demands, and fighting for victories that are only within the boundaries of what the system has to offer? It is, if the goal is only to make gains, that is, to focus on outcomes. This was certainly the dominant model that grew out of the 1960s. However, when organizers moved to the left in the 1970s and also began to incorporate feminism or anti-racist politics as part of their ideologies, there was a shift in emphasis. The process of organizing became important. The analysis was that organizing for specific gains was important, but at the same time, it was also important that people developed an understanding of how the system worked, who held power, and why it was necessary to build toward long-term change. Basically, change began to happen due to the actions of local people who had learned to act and who also understood the context and the limits imposed by that context. Further, the processes through which this occurred became highly valued. Thus, democratic opportunities and participative forms of decision-making had to be present. The emphasis on process implies that social change is a long-term process that involves shifts in ideas and analysis and the creation of alternative democratic spaces. I will now turn to a discussion of models to examine the links between theory and practice.

STRATEGY AND MODELS

As we have seen, community practices come from two different traditions of social change strategy. The first comes out of a social action tradition and involves exerting pressure on specific targets—governments, corporations, etc.—in order to force these bodies to implement some kind of change in policy or behaviour. The impact of these changes improves the lives of people at the local level. Implementing a program that redistributes wealth (desirable but currently unlikely) is an example. The second tradition is the creation of a service or a program or a developmental process at the local level that can ameliorate a problem. This is the action-development dichotomy. However, returning to goals raised by Rubin and Rubin, neither of these inherently expands democratic or learning opportunities. Social action work may be carried out by advocacy agencies or professional activists who do not necessarily organize people to participate in their campaigns. Similarly, service provision or development can be controlled by professionals and may not necessarily involve direct participation of people at the local level in the process of organization and management of these services. Both the action and developmental approaches can provide opportunities for involvement of citizens and can create democratic structures through which people can shape local processes and organizations. The links between social change and community organization are complex and cannot be understood only by listing characteristics. Both outcomes and processes have importance. Within practices there are elements of social change activities alongside other elements that reproduce inequalities and hierarchical relations, as we shall see.

MODELS OF PRACTICE

It was not until the late 1960s that academics, particularly in schools of social work, expanded the literature and tried to examine the community organizing practice systematically. As Rothman points out in his autobiographical essay (1999), this attempt reflected innovation in the field and new contestation and mobilization of poor people. During the 1970s, several readers were published in the United States to examine emerging practices. Perhaps the most enduring of these texts has been *Strategies of Community Organization: A Book of Readings*. This book has gone through many editions, but the core framework remains the same. It is based on an essay by Jack Rothman, "Three Models of Community Organization Practice," published for the first time in 1968. These models were not conceived in abstraction but were constructed from Rothman's observation of the actual practice of his students. The durability of these models reflects some of the continuity in practice; however, they have to be read as a way to identify similarities in a world of blurred boundaries. I will use Rothman's work as a starting point to enter into a discussion of approaches, models, and assumptions in community organization practice.

Rothman sets out three distinct models, but acknowledges that in the world of practice they are not mutually exclusive. The three models are locality development, social planning, and social action. The advantage to this classification is that they enable us to examine the underlying assumptions and social change strategies implicit in each, such as the relationship and analysis of social power and the implication of these understandings for the processes involved in organizing.

The *locality development approach* is based on assumptions of common interest among groups in society. It assumes that, through this common interest, social problems can be solved by bringing together representatives of as many groups as possible, each contributing in their own way. Community change can be pursued "through broad participation of a wide spectrum of people at the local community level" (Rothman, 1999, p. 23). It includes the diverse interests of the local community and emphasizes social processes. For example, if hunger is the problem, a food bank can be set up through a process of consensus-building among service providers. Conflict is absent from this approach, and it is assumed that common interest overrides differentials of power, income, and wealth at the local level. We will see later how this model has become increasingly important in recent years and how its assumption of common interest acts to maintain the status quo and either directly or indirectly supports ruling relations. At the same time, it is a model that supports direct involvement of citizens and confers responsibility on them for local activity. This is a strength, but it is the direction of this participation that remains problematic.

The *social planning model* is technocratic, emphasizing a top-down approach to problem-solving. It looks for technical solutions and believes in rational tools and the expertise of professionals. The planning process begins with organizations that are located outside the community, and its intervention is in the form of specific services or programs designed to meet particular needs. It may involve residents in the process but does not usually transfer power to them to manage the programs produced. This model has a long history in social welfare dating back to the 1930s when charities tried to coordinate both fund-raising and allocation and continues in the work of Centraid/United Way and other planning bodies. We will not explore this model here, concentrating instead on those approaches that focus on processes at the local level.

Rothman's third model, *social action*, promotes changes in power relations and direct action of a segment of the community that is without power and resources. This approach gained a following among activists in the 1960s, a period of challenges to social policies and the social order. Conflict is central, and interest and power relations are explicit; they are clearly named in this model. The oppressed, the poor, etc., should organize themselves with the support of community organizers and challenge those with power. The goal is for them to gain greater resources and a stronger voice. In the 1960s and 1970s, when these approaches were developed, students, workers, women, and racial and cultural minorities mobilized and demanded a variety of social and economic changes. Direct action was the currency to obtain these demands.

I will focus on two categories of community practice—community development derived from Rothman's locality development and community action or social action. Minkler and Wallerstein (1999) use a similar approach contrasting what they describe as consensus and conflict, arguing that the community development tradition is derived from a consensus model, while social action is based primarily on a conflict model. In the next two chapters, I will discuss both of these in more detail. As I have argued in an essay co-authored with Robert Fisher (2000) and in the first part of this chapter, there has been a shift from an action orientation, which was the most prevalent form of practice in the 1960s and 1970s, to the development approach, which has become more significant since the 1980s. One

of the key differences between these models is their basic understanding of power and conflict. The action perspective acknowledges
and challenges power, believing that the role of organizing is to help
those without power build a voice to articulate their interests. In contrast, the development approach aims to build social consensus.

Stoecker (2001) links theoretical perspectives with the models of
practice. He argues that the development and action models are
rooted in two different theories—functionalism and conflict.
Functionalism argues that society has a basic equilibrium or balance;
in maintaining it, people fall into roles in which they fit themselves,
and any movement is through individual action or personal change.
Further, all people in society share a common interest. Thus, poor
people need opportunity and cooperation and not power as a means
of escaping poverty. Conflict theory, Stoecker argues, "sees society as
divided particularly between corporations and workers, men and
women, and whites and people of color" (p. 3). Conflict provides the
means of seeking social change, and power is the key issue. The
action model is concerned with groups building power to contest
issues that affect their lives. The development approach, on the other
hand, seeks change through consensus-building between those with
differing interests and power.

The importance of models is to pull some of the commonalities
out of the complexities of practice and present them in a systematic
way. However, practice does not begin with models. Most people
toiling in the community are thrown into situations or jobs (organizing by the seats of their pants, as one organizer described it) and
figuring out what they are doing as events develop. The real problem
with this is that practitioners have difficulty reflecting upon their
work and examining the contradictions that emerge. Models can help
in that process because they make the underlying assumptions
explicit and suggest actions that can be derived from them. For
example, an organizer may be working toward consensus-building
and partnership at the local level and then wonder why she/he is
having trouble getting the poor people of a community to represent
themselves and articulate their demands. Using consensus between
people with unequal power and interests make it difficult for disen-

franchised groups to have an independent voice. Thus, if the goal is to help a group gain some control over local institutions, then starting with a partnership/consensus model would not be the way to reach this end.

There are several limitations to model building. The complexities and overlaps are not easily represented, nor is the movement from one type of practice to another over the life of an organization. For example, an effective social action organization can make gains such as revitalizing a deteriorated neighbourhood, and then act to protect these gains by excluding outsiders or institutions deemed as undesirable (NIMBY—Not In My Back Yard). Similarly, the movement from action to service provision is a common transition. Organizing is used to gain a voice for a group excluded from local politics and processes, but once the group has achieved success and resources, it can become part of a community network of service provision and not take the organizing further. Models, seen from the point of view of practice, do not represent these shifts and transitions.

Further, models lack a historical dimension that can situate the evolution of organizing activities within particular contexts. The question is why certain approaches predominate in specific periods while in other times others might co-exist and are less visible or play a reduced social and political role. To understand this, an analysis of the social and historical contexts is vital. Here we enter into the complex interaction between the forces of the wider context to shape practice and the power of human agency to override outside pressures. Fisher (1999) describes this tension:

> Certainly issues of human agency-leadership, ideology, daily choices regarding strategies and tactics and so forth—all play a critical role in the life of any effort, but the larger context heavily influences what choices are available, what ideology or goals are salient, and what approaches seem appropriate or likely to succeed. By its very nature, history puts the actions and work of individuals into a larger framework, interweaving the local with the more global, the particular

with the broader trends, events, and developments in society. (p. 344)

The context can include a variety of factors such as the balance of social forces—the strength of contesting groups in the society, such as the working class with its unions or other social movements. Another factor is the strategy of the state and the types of programs that follow from its orientation. Wider political and social alignments also play an important role in shaping the possibilities for community organizations. Into these forces organizers intervene, using their creativity and energy, often defined by the resources available for the organizing activities. This in turn shapes the choices for an organization whose survival may be contingent upon a limited range of possibilities dictated by state programs and policies. At the same time, the power and forces mobilized from below can limit and shape state policies. It is difficult for these forces to be represented in models, but the models themselves can be situated historically— when they developed and how and what forces shaped their role and their degree of success.

Another difficulty with models is that the basic vision of social change is not made explicit. For example, can the locality development model used by Rothman be considered as part of an approach that promotes basic radical change? If so, then how? There is a tendency to identify the social action model or community action as the only model that contributes to progressive social change, because of its conflictual stance and its explicit critique of social and political power. It is viewed as a means of pressuring those with power for specific concessions. But the practice itself is far more complex.

There are fundamental questions to be asked of the models: what are the underlying connections between the practices themselves and the processes of social change? Are there theories and traditions of social change that are implicit in different models of practice? Further, what do we understand about the process of social change, and how is this process linked to practice? These core questions are central in the chapters that follow.

CHAPTER THREE

SOCIAL ACTION AND ITS LEGACY FOR SOCIAL CHANGE

The legacies of community organizing practice are complex. As I discussed in the previous chapter, neither the development nor the action models are necessarily directed at progressive social change. Both have potential if used along with a value base and a strategic understanding of what each can accomplish. In this chapter, I will explore the community action approach by examining several perspectives. I will start with the work of Saul Alinsky, the American community organizer who popularized the method and its strategies. He, more than anyone else, named the process and envisioned the neighbourhood as a place for organizing. All of the organizers who followed learned from him. I will follow this with a discussion of the contribution of the North American New Left. Although their efforts in the late 1960s did not produce lasting outcomes, their ideas and experiments, particularly in new forms of participation by citizens and direct democracy, have influenced social and political movements to this day and have shaped experiments in building local alternative practices. The women's movement took the new practices further and added the personal and political dimensions. A variety of social movements followed, building on these themes and playing their own variations. We can see many radical and social traditions growing out of social movements and community organizing, while, at the same time, there are many questions and contradictions. The legacy is not always clear.

ALINSKY AND THE RISE OF SOCIAL ACTION ORGANIZING

Social or community action organizing has a long and almost mythical history. It is the story of building opposition to the dominant social structures, challenging power. It is the story of the oppressed and poor making claims on the rich and powerful. Like any other mythology, the actual history is more complex. When I began my work in community organizing, the biggest name and most famous organizer was Saul Alinsky. He was a pioneer, an innovator, a fast-talking, self-promoting organizer who began his work in the working-class neighbourhoods of ethnic Chicago in the 1940s. Because of his influence, I shall start with his contribution to organizing and then look at the way his approach was reshaped by the New Left of the late 1960s and early 1970s. Then I will examine the contributions of the feminist movement. I have grouped these three together because I will argue that, although each has its own independent legacy, they each contributed important ideas which can be synthesized to bring a broad-based understanding of the processes that link social change and community organizing.

Although there are many examples of pressure group organizing before Alinsky, he was the one who put in order a systematic practice of community/neighbourhood organizing, was successful in many projects, was well-known both in and outside of the United States, and influenced many organizers who followed. I will not present either his biography or an account of his organizing work, but will concentrate on some key features, lessons, and debates that have emerged from it.

Alinsky, a product of the old left, more social democratic than communist, carried on the traditions of the labour movement. He believed that reform was possible within the structures and processes of capitalism and promoted a pragmatic approach to social change that emphasized the potential of the poor and powerless to make gains through the processes of community organization. For him, power was the essential element; this power was built through organization, and momentum was achieved through making concrete gains or winning victories. He (1971) wrote:

> Change comes from power, and power comes from organization. In order to act, people must get together.... The organizer knows that his [sic] biggest job is to give the people the feeling that they can do something, that while they may accept that organization means power, they have to experience this idea in action. The organizer's job is to begin to build confidence and hope in the idea of organization and thus in the people themselves: to win limited victories, each of which will build confidence. (pp. 113–14)

In other words, large numbers of people acting collectively could force changes, could make concrete gains.

Alinsky was committed to a pragmatic approach and spoke against an organizer holding an "ideology":

> What kind of ideology, if any, can an organizer have ... he does not have a fixed truth—truth to him [sic] is relative and changing; *everything* to him is relative and changing. He is a political relativist...To the extent that he is free from the shackles of dogma, he can respond to the realities of the widely different situations our society presents. In the end he has one conviction—a belief that if the people have the power to act, in the long run they will, most of the time, reach the right decisions. (Alinsky, 1971, pp. 10–11)

Alinsky, himself, was larger than life and by the 1960s was becoming an urban legend. He was called into many cities to help with the building of organizations in poor communities. He was often vilified publicly by local political establishments. The organizations he helped create were set up to mobilize people, win issues, and make gains. However, the results were more complex than the rhetoric and images. Some of the organizations had relatively short lives, five or six years (Fisher 1994), and those that survived beyond that became transformed from confrontational and activist to managers of social and economic programs. For example, one of the better known, more highly acclaimed organizations, The Woodlawn Organization (TWO), in Chicago "became just another business in the community, a nonprofit business almost as removed from many of Woodlawn's problems and needs as the profit oriented businesses" (Fisher, 1994, p. 144).

Alinsky's legacy is important despite its contradictions. One contribution was the legitimization and making explicit the role of a community organizer as a form of "professional" activity. He not only described the functions of this work but also believed in the training of organizers, drawing them from the ranks of local leadership. His organization, the Industrial Areas Foundation (IAF), trained many who went on to become leaders in community and social struggles. Another lesson that is certainly not unique to Alinsky but was strongly promoted by him is that the source of community power is in large numbers of people acting through an organization. This lesson is self-evident at one level, but it is easily forgotten. In recent years in both Canada and the United States, there has been a shift from an emphasis on mobilization of large numbers of people to one of representation of people through coalitions of organizations. The loss of this perspective has contributed in part to a weakening of opposition movements. One can be critical of the form of the organization that Alinsky used, but this basic principle is sound: the creation of popular organizations is the key to building power. In contrast to more generalized protest activity, organizations provide continuity, structure, and a means of sustaining activity.

Although it is easy to criticize Alinsky's approach retrospectively, it is important to remember that he promoted a path-breaking method and opened up many new possibilities. We need to see his contribution as being shaped and supported by other national and international social and political movements, which generated popular interest and a more progressive and optimistic context. His major successes were linked to the anti-fascist and union movement during the late 1930s and early 1940s and the struggle for civil rights in the 1960s (Fisher, 1994). Alinsky's method was to use organization to get those outside of the power structure closer to it in order to negotiate specific concessions. As well, in the periods of his greatest activity, the state played an interventionist role supporting social development; therefore, it was easier to get support for the organizing and to secure victories. The combination of pragmatism and mobilization within acceptable boundaries combined with a confrontational style created the contradictory image of Alinsky as organizer who was simultaneously radical and liberal.

Turning to criticisms, one can begin with the consequences of this pragmatism. Alinsky and those who have written about him emphasize the necessity of winnable issues as a way of demonstrating the capacity and power of the community organization. What if an issue is not immediately winnable, particularly at the local level? Does this imply that it is to not be tackled? How does an organization confront fundamental economic and social issues such as welfare, poverty, etc., if the issues that are selected are based on their winnability and their potential to contribute to the building of the organization? In practice, change is defined within narrow parameters. This begins to shape the nature of the organization itself. I would argue further that controlled change within pre-existing limits is the outcome, and, despite the militant tactics, the actual demands do not pose a threat to the basic relations of power and wealth. Organizing becomes channelled in a direction that can be supported by foundations and churches, that improves local conditions but that remains well within the bounds of small-scale reform that can be organizationally managed and negotiated.

Linked to this problem are the inherent constraints of localism. Neighbourhood organizations that promote local improvement and do not build alliances that can challenge broader issues remain isolated, and their ability to build opposition is inherently limited. I describe this as "power within." What about power beyond the local?

Alinsky recognized this limitation. In his book *Rules for Radicals* (1971), he argued for the use of proxy campaigns as a way to use shares in corporations to confront them and to democratize control of large businesses. At the same time, he wanted to broaden his constituency to include the middle class. Neither of these came to fruition. Some campaigns have used proxies to enter into annual meetings of corporations and challenge them on a variety of issues, but corporate structures and concentration of ownership mitigate against the possibility of small share-holders influencing the direction of large companies. Thus, even with the recognition of the problem of the limits of localism, Alinsky and his organizations never really got beyond it.

The idea of training organizers is an important contribution, but it is flawed in some basic ways. Alinsky trained effective organizers in his own tough "macho" image. These organizers were central to any initiative and provided more than leadership; they helped initiate organizations and played a controlling role in them. However, one can question the power and accountability of the organizer. The organizing process puts the organizer in the centre, and his/her credibility rests with his/her ability to recruit leaders and members. The functions of the organizer include building the organization, identifying leaders, and helping them to build skills and local visibility. Local issues act as a way to recruit people into the process. In theory, the organizer works himself/herself out of a job as the leaders they have groomed achieve the capacity necessary to carry out organizing functions. In addition, the role of the organizer is supposed to be to suggest options and choices for the organization; decisions are reached through an internal democratic process. The reality is more complex. Organizers have a lot of control, particularly in the early stages. As the organization matures, organizers are still there and work closely with leaders to shape agendas and direction. The problem is the lack of accountability by the organizer to the leadership and members. In practice the program and approaches to organizing are predefined, and participation is a vehicle to sanction the choices already put in place through the initiative of the organizer. I am not arguing that democracy is an easy process but, rather, that the organizer has a lot of power in shaping and controlling the process. The role is not clearly acknowledged, and the organizer stands both inside and outside the organization at the same time. A related issue is the character of the organizer himself (I use "him" deliberately here). Alinsky-style organizing, perhaps inadvertently, is based on the "great man" approach to history. Being an organizer requires sacrifice, long hours, little commitment to family life, and personal charisma. I have presented students with National Film Board films and books by and about Alinsky. The reaction, particularly among women students, is that they cannot possibly become that type of practitioner—larger than life, a dynamic leader. We discuss the reality of effective organizing work—the day-to-day grind, the multitude of small tasks, the relation-building processes with citizens at the local level. Although Alinsky includes this mundanity, his persona overwhelms it. The dedication he demanded is far beyond what most people are willing, or able, to give.

Linda Stout (1996) has written a more realistic portrait of an organizer. She describes her transformation from growing up in a poor southern White family in Appalachia with little formal education, to becoming an effective community organizer. She acknowledges all of the difficulties and struggles, the self-doubt she experienced on the way, and the role of supportive relationships in helping her through the difficult changes. Her example is far more encouraging and realistic. Her writing and style has been influenced by the changes in politics and ideologies introduced by feminism. To contrast her story with that of Alinsky is to confront the mystique perpetuated among male organizers that only those who are charismatic leaders should become involved in community organizing.

Another challenge to Alinsky's approach is the question of organization and organization-building. He believed that peoples' organizations are a necessary component in a strategy for social change. Here we come to the central difficulty and a major debate in community organization theory and practice. Is building an organization the most effective way to promote social change? If not, what are the other options? If so, what kind of organization will fit the bill? Alinsky believed in organizations that have a formal process and complex structure, which require maintenance and a permanent source of funding. In addition, he felt that action on several different local issues was useful in building the structure since it recruited people who had an interest and a stake in working on specific issues. One can question whether maintaining a structure is really worthwhile, given both the resources and time necessary to do that and that the mobilization is not necessarily enhanced because the organization is in place. Further, the formal structures used by Alinsky and others provide the basis for a shift in orientation from a social action strategy to one providing service or developmental work. Organizations require support to manage their own structures; thus, they are pushed toward finding funds, usually from sources that provide support for more traditional activities, such as service provision. Because the organization structure has the capacity to manage budgets and programs, this indirectly becomes the seed of a process of demobilization.

In an article I wrote with Glenn Drover in 1979, we argued that one of the faults of Alinsky-style organizing was that the process of organizational maintenance took too much energy and resources. We put forward a counter position, drawing on the work of Cloward and Piven (1977). A strategy of mobilization rather than organizational building requires a small group of "political friends," who carry out organizing work at the local level. Such a small group of organizers does not require the same level of resources and can embark on periodic educational campaigns and mobilization with far less dependence on outside resources. I have come back to this position over the years, as I have seen excellent political campaigns launched at the community level based on direct mobilization of citizens and *ad hoc* coalitions of organizations. In the next section, we will revisit the organizational question, less from the point of view of the debate on organization versus mobilization than on the direct democratic perspectives emerging from the New Left and the women's movement.

The Alinsky approach provides a starting point for a discussion of community organizing. It legitimated community action organizing as a vehicle for social change. It brought the energies of the social movements of his time into neighbourhoods and provided another vehicle through which people could make claims for improvements in their lives. In a sense, he took progressive politics and brought them into the community. This was a step forward, as previous to that a charity and service model prevailed there. However, his method had limits, provoked debates, and caused problems for the continued mobilization of neighbourhood activism. Those who followed him borrowed from Alinsky, but put their own mark on organizing, providing a continuity, a layering of approaches, rather than a break from his legacy.

COMMUNITY AS SOCIAL CHANGE: THE NEW LEFT AND SOCIAL MOVEMENTS

As I discussed in Chapter 1, the wave of student protest of the 1960s shaped my own consciousness, more in terms of stance and attitude than in terms of specific analysis and theory. As I became more involved in community organizing in graduate school and in Montreal, I met many activists who had graduated from activities in the student movement and the New Left to struggles in the community. They were armed with an analysis of the wider society, experience in student politics, energy, and dedication, and they found sources of support from government and private foundations. In both Canada and the United States, activists sought new forms of organization and new ways to link their analysis to practice. Many of their experiments did not succeed in the short term, but in the longer term, their practices and values have had an impact. The ideas of the student movement took hold in a variety of activities and social movements that followed such as the women's, ecology, and peace movements, as well as in many neighbourhood organizing projects.

In order to understand the innovations of the New Left and the connection between community organizing and social change inherent in its politics, it is necessary to contrast the New and the Old Left. One difficulty is that the New Left did not have a coherent ideology, and the dominant voice shifted over time. There were two distinct periods in New Left politics in both Canada and the United States: the first occurred between 1962–68, and the second from

1969 into the 1970s. The former period is ideologically more open, while the latter, in many instances, was shaped by revolutionary Marxist perspectives. In the United States after 1968, greater social polarization, violence, and repression led to a New Left absorbed in the politics of violence and revolution and interested in Third World struggles; consequently, it placed less emphasis on the values and experiments of the earlier period. This does not mean that these earlier practices disappeared. Many stayed the course and continued to work in communities, building organizations, running campaigns, and creating projects, but these did not share the media spotlight trained on violent confrontations.

The New Left differed in several ways from the Old, which had its roots in the Russian Revolution, the Great Depression, World War II and its aftermath of rebuilding, and subsequent Cold War politics. Those in the traditional Old Left believed in reform from above and in the potential of economic growth and technology to produce reform and ameliorate social and economic conditions (Breines 1989). The New Left of the early 1960s did not have much of an affinity for these traditions, but was influenced far more by pacifism and anarchism. As Breines (1989) states:

> The vision of the New Left, developed in affluence rather than depression and fascism, was of a cornu-copia of possibilities. A social system in which everyone participated equally seemed desirable and possible; class was not critical to its vision.... the New Left became interested in culture and hegemony: concepts central for understanding the hold which advanced capitalism had on people's consciousness. The old left was preoccupied with "objective conditions" of revolution, while the New Left highlighted the importance of "subjective conditions." (p. 16)

In addition, the activists of the New Left were based, at least initially, in the university. They were a generation who lived a combination of economic stability and personal alienation. Universities were in the process of rapid growth, and students critiqued their educational experience as one that served the corporate elite. New ideas grew out of these experiences.

One of the most influential intellectuals of the period was the sociologist C. Wright Mills. Central in his writings were the link of the personal to the political and the notion of a radical democracy shaped by face-to-face decision-making. These ideas were developed in the years that followed and became central to the differences between the Old and New Lefts. The belief in the direct participation of people in decisions that affected them was to have an enormous impact on the approaches to community organizing (Miller, 1987).

Thus, the processes of democracy involved the creation of community for those who shared a common cause. The key concept was "pre-figuration," which Breines (1989) defines as follows:

> The effort to build community, to create and prefigure in lived action and behavior the desired society, the emphasis on means and not ends, the spontaneous utopian experiments that developed in the midst of action while working toward the ultimate goal of a free and democratic society, were among the most important contributions of the movements of the 1960s. (p. xiv)

From this, community organizing followed two directions. The first was similar to Alinsky's program, focussing on power and social issues. The second involved a radical democratic process based on face-to-face relations. Richard Flacks, one of the leaders of Students for a Democratic Society (SDS) argued, in 1965, that there was a tension between the two types of goals, one involving "a redistribution of wealth and power" and the other "an attempt to achieve 'community' to reach levels of intimacy and directness with others ... to be self-expressive, to be free" (cited in Miller, 1987, p. 238). It was not enough to fight for material gains, since social processes had to touch the personal:

> The search for and/or struggle to defend community,
> both the "sense" of community and actual community
> institutions, becomes political in the context of the
> changes that capitalism has brought in the everyday
> life of the individual—changes characterized by lack
> of control at work school and play; impersonality and
> competition in all areas of life. (Breines, 1989, p. 7)

In the creation of new community-based organizations in the years that followed, the emphasis on participation and process was the source of the democratic innovation that shaped many new practices. One can criticize prefiguration for being utopian and, therefore, not something easily incorporated into the daily struggles for specific gains which, by necessity, are shaped by more pragmatic practices. However, in its refinement over the years, the quest for democracy in the everyday helped shape many new forms of organizing and bequeathed a powerful legacy.

The New Left also challenged the concept of agency in a way that gets to the core of its difference from the Old Left. The Old Left believed that the working class, through unions and political parties, in either revolutionary or parliamentary incarnations, was the vehicle for basic change and that the class struggle was the motor that drove social reform. Following the critique of Mills, Herbert Marcuse, and others, the New Left saw the working class as integrated into North American materialism and the consumer society (Miller, 1987). The period of affluence after World War II had allowed industrial workers to make many gains and created relative stability. It was not uncommon to find unionized workers living in suburbs and enjoying the benefits of consumerism Unions had became a vehicle for the protection of the narrow material interests of their members. The New Left in the United States did not see the trade union movement or the political party it supported—the Democratic Party—as having any commitment to radical social change. These organizations themselves were hierarchical and did not support the radical democracy that the New Left sought. In Canada, the New Left was divided on this question. As Laxer (1996) points out, many followed the orientation of activists from the United States:

> Youthful activists sought to politicize the poor in community organizing programs that were replicas of programs south of the border—as though Canada had no political traditions or unique social characteristics and values. (pp. 149–50)

However, others challenged the social democratic New Democratic Party (NDP) from within. In 1969, a group of young activists from English Canada, the Waffle group, prepared a manifesto that promoted Canadian nationalism and challenged American control of Canadian culture and economy. The clash of political cultures and ideas eventually led to the expulsion of the Waffle, but their ideas influenced the party and contributed to a rebirth of Canadian nationalism (Laxer, 1996). Thus, both the ideas from the United States with its anti-party, direct action perspective and the traditions of a parliamentary social democratic party shaped the practices and strategies of the New Left in Canada.

The question of the role of the working class as an agent of social change is difficult to resolve in theory and was even more complex in practice. The New Left in the United States witnessed and participated in the civil rights movement in the early 1960s. Black communities in the south challenged segregation and exclusion and won concessions through direct action. At the same time, students in both Canada and the United States were engaged in a struggle against the "multiversity," which they believed served corporate interests. They demanded a voice and control of these institutions. The common ground was the concept of participatory democracy. The struggle for social and economic justice—which the New Left as well as the Old held as fundamentally important—could not be carried out unless the institutions themselves were fundamentally democratized. The majority of people, the New Left believed, had no real voice and lived in the pretense of democracy. The quest for power to shape their own lives and the institutions that touched them could bring together many disenfranchised groups (Miller, 1987). The process of democratizing all aspects of society was the means and strategy to challenge the wider society. Even with its attempt to engage in the NDP, the New Left held to these basic values.

The leading journal of the New Left in Canada was *Our Generation*. Founded as a journal for the disarmament movement in the early 1960s, it reflected the development of the voice of the New Left as it evolved into anarchist and left libertarian thought and analysis. An editorial in 1969 articulated the rejection of prevailing political and social institutions as having the potential to change society and posited agency as a broad-based radical movement. The editors wrote:

> The traditional agencies of political change are failing, and so have the older definitions of politics.... We have no alternative but to withdraw our allegiance from the machines of the electoral process, from the institutions of "representative democracy" like parliaments to forego the magical rite of voting for our freedom, and resume our own initiatives before liberal corporatism asphyxiates us. We are now in a period of transition like the system itself, in which we will seek to unite radicals, in new forms of resistance and counter-institutional building... we wish to create a political movement of people with the capacity to determine their own lives. (*Our Generation*, 1969, p. 15)

The editorial went on to call for the building of an "Extra-Parliamentary Opposition" that would bring together people and groups who shared a common critique and minimal program. Although it required a broad-based movement, the leadership of the more radical wing would come from:

> the new left student and youth movement which demands that producers control what they produce using the operational principles of ... "participatory or direct democracy".... They seek to organise new

centres of power among ethnic and racial minorities, urban and rural workers, youth, the poor, and other groups on a neighbourhood and work level. (*Our Generation*, 1969, p. 16)

Thus, the New Left understood leadership and agency in different terms than the Old Left did. It did not believe in social change through parliamentary channels, and it did not confer on one group—the working class—the "leadership" role in social struggles. Building power and gaining a voice was inclusive and needed the participation of many.

Following these beliefs, some activists in the American New Left decided to move off campus and engage in community organizing in low-income communities, as a new way to extend its political action. The SDS set up the Economic Research and Action Project (ERAP) in 1963. Its brochure stated:

> We have chosen to work with people who most desperately need alternatives to poverty and economic voicelessness, and to devote ourselves to the development of community organization capable of achieving a better deal for the poor in a democratic fashion. (quoted in Breines, 1989, p. 125)

One of the most committed and effective organizers from that time, Susan Jeffery, reflected on her experience:

> I wanted to organize people, I wanted to organize a movement. I mean, on some level it was stupid: we were going to organize the "lumpen," it wasn't Marxist at all, we were going after people who were totally disenfranchised and disempowered and disorganized at a personal level. But we wanted to be independent. We wanted to have a major impact on American society. So we had to carve out an arena in which there wasn't yet an organization. (quoted in Miller, 1987, p. 190)

Thus, the New Left sought new constituencies, particularly those who had not benefitted from the post-war boom. In an essay reflecting on the experience of the SDS, Todd Gitlin argued that the poor had many unmet needs, were least tied to the dominant values of the system, and, therefore, had the potential to work for radical social change (in Tedori, 1969). The New Left saw community organizing as having the potential to bring poor people together to work for a common project—the transformation of society. Tedori (1969) summarizes the position as follows:

> the movements suggest a political-organizational praxis which is based on the following criteria (a) decentralization and multiplicity of structures and actions which serves the movements, and not vice versa; (b) direct method of self-government at all levels, rather than delegated authority and responsibility; (c) abolition of institutionalized political bureaucracies and of a division of political labor between leaders and those who carry out the leadership's policy; (d) nonexclusion. (p. 37)

Each project was to have autonomy with local leadership, and the hope was that, through the building of local power and a long-term social and political vision, alliances for radical social change could come together.

Fisher (1994) summarizes the principles that guided the organizing efforts.

1. Be a catalyst not a leader. The role of the organizer is to facilitate social processes and not lead the community. Local people are to play that role.

2. The key slogan of the period was "let the people decide."

3. Develop loose organizational structures that can maximize participation of the people; the emphasis is on consensus decision-making.

4. Establish places in the community free of external
    restraints, a "community union" that belongs to
    neighbourhood people.
5. Develop indigenous leaders. This principle is cou-
    pled to the second and sees the organizer as a
    person who is in the background, so that local
    people can represent themselves.
6. Create personal relationships. The organizer is to
    build "Supportive, noncompetitive relations
    between organizers and community people [that]
    would prefigure future ways of relating in the new
    truly democratic society." (pp. 109-10)

New Left organizers carried these principles into the field. In the
United States, they attempted to build local organizations in urban
ghettoes. They did not find the reality as easy as the theory. Internal
democratic processes were time-consuming and tiring, while the
issues they could manage at the local level seemed trivial. The community union approach organized people around specific grievances
such as problems of garbage, traffic, or late welfare checks (Breines,
1989). Tom Hayden (1988) describes the work of one project in
Newark, New Jersey, where neighbourhood blocks were organized
to work on local issues and support the development of local leaders.
He states:

> In a few weeks, we had 250 people meeting in about
> fifteen block groups. We began knitting them into a
> neighborhood-wide organization so that people from
> each block could see their problems in larger perspec-
> tive. We held weekly meetings of block leaders, which
> led to a neighborhood leadership body. We opened a
> storefront office on a seven day basis. Soon our
> mimeos were pouring out leaflets announcing meet-
> ings and demonstrations or outlining in simple terms
> such subjects as tenants' rights and where to get legal
> aid. (p. 132)

Many of these efforts met with initial success, but they were hard to sustain. Further, with the escalation of the Vietnam War and urban revolt in American ghettoes in the late 1960s, organizing efforts were derailed. However, their principal ideas and methods influenced many who stayed in the field.

In Canada, the organizing followed similar patterns with young people working among the poor. Poor peoples' organizations were founded in major cities, along with new "counter-institutions" such as community clinics. A nation-wide government program, the Company of Young Canadians (CYC), was launched in the mid-1960s to give young people an outlet for their newly acquired social activism in support of grassroots community organizing. It had a controversial history, balanced tensely between promoting social change and falling under the control of the bureaucracy in Ottawa (Brodhead, Goodings, and Brodhead, 1997).

The move by government into community organizing through this program did not go unchallenged from within the New Left. For instance, one New Left leader chastised another's participation in CYC by reminding him that the state would not finance the revolution (Daly, 1970). This tension between using opportunities that were available even if they presented political dangers versus an uncompromising revolutionary stance differentiated those who felt that it was possible to make gains by working in and through "the system" and those who wanted to stay the leftist course. Once entered into the struggles of a local community, it became much more difficult to ignore the pragmatic tugs of specific problems that had to be solved. For those who held to the radical side of the debate, this was a conflict that could not be easily resolved in the daily life of organizing.

Another tension emerged with the practice of participatory democracy. The New Left was anti-leadership and believed that "the people" should make decisions, but community organizers came from a privileged background, were educated, and had time to reflect on what they were doing. "The people" were brought in afterwards; they were to be organized. There was a real power differential created by a culture that gave greater credibility to those who were articulate and educated. In practice, power was informal and hidden, and there was little formal accountability for the organizers. Richard Rothstein suggested that the way to solve this problem was to put "formal powers in the hands of community people, in other words, reinstituting formal structure" (cited in Breines, 1989, p. 81). This lesson was learned, and, as practice developed in the years that followed, structures were put in place that acknowledged the role of organizers and demanded their accountability.

By the late 1960s, women were beginning to challenge some of the patriarchal practices in the New Left, especially since they tended to be the most effective organizers and most local issues sprang from the domestic sphere (Breines, 1989). At the same time, the most visible organizers tended to be men. The developing feminist consciousness provided a natural bridge between woman organizers and poor women in the community who shared oppression. These themes will be developed later in this chapter (see p. 98).

The New Left also raised the limits of localism. Critics charged that community organizing could not break through its local focus and, therefore, could not build a radical program that would place the class question at its centre. Further, the central issue of redistribution of wealth could not be challenged from the local sphere (Breines, 1989). This issue is not unlike the critique of Alinsky-style organizing, but takes the question further. The New Left's emerging Marxist analysis with its focus on class raised difficult questions for those engaged in local work. The long-term goals of fundamental social change were shared by those working in the community as well as by those advocating workers' revolution, but community organizing was often trapped in the day-to-day demands of working locally. This often clouded the long-term vision. Community organizers argued that local organizing raised the basic question of democracy, unmasked the realities of how power operated, and provided the opportunity for direct participation and power. These in turn created the conditions which, according to Fruchter and Kramer, "create, then enlarge, a space in which the possible alternatives can be developed, and the possible challenge to the status quo can be kept alive" (quoted in Breines, 1989). This debate is the central one, perhaps more important now when opposition forces to a common right wing and neo-liberal agenda are weak. Local organizing might not win great battles, but it can create autonomous democratic places from which mobilization and political organizing are possible. Many projects of this period were innovative and laid foundations for initiatives that followed. However, the actual organizing, day-to-day, did not depart from the Alinsky approach. Building local power by means of a popular organization and gaining concessions through the use of pressure tactics were the common features. However, there were differences. The organizers did not define themselves as professionals but as movement activists. They tried to share, as much as possible, the communities and situations of the people whom they were trying to organize. The New Left believed strongly that the organizations they founded were part of a wider social movement working for fundamental social change; therefore, political education—exposing basic inequalities and injustices—was part of the agenda. The movement (as it was called then) had many components, but shared common aims and analysis; organizing locally was only one part. The way that loose networks would come together was never made clear.

Organizing was directed outward. It was a process of societal change; local gains, although not incidental, were a means to the end and less important than the longer struggle. Thus, the organizers, in particular, identified with a larger process and were connected to the international movement that was blossoming in the 1960s. The organizational form was supposed to be non-hierarchical, and participation was to be encouraged in an open process, in contrast to the highly structured Alinsky-type organizations. The New Left raised the organizational question not only in theory but also in practice, with an experimental energy that tried to expand democratic participation into all aspects of daily life.

Perhaps the most important legacies of the period were the two related concepts that shaped the practice: prefiguration and parallel organization. The belief that people had to "live the revolution" shaped direct democratic participation, not only in community organizations but also in struggles on campus. It was not uncommon for students to hold mass decision-making meetings open to all those who wanted to participate. Granted this was chaotic, but it extended democratic process, and this was the objective. The experimentation with new democratic forms was carried forward into the building of "parallel" organizations that integrated the organizational approach with a service. In Montreal in the late 1960s, community clinics were established in working-class communities and in areas where the counter-culture gathered. The leadership was an alliance of young professionals influenced by the student left and local community activists (Shragge, 1990). Parallel institutions were democratic, jointly controlled by local citizens and radical professionals who were contributing to both the provision of a service and the opening of democratic space. At the same time, workers, volunteers, and users of these services continued to participate in a variety of political and social struggles. Service was not divorced from political action.

The organizing efforts initiated by the New Left on both sides of the border in the 1960s represent the beginning of a new type of activism. A decade later, many saw the end of this brief period of youthful radicalism. In the United States, violence and repression polarized the movement, as many advocated armed resistance, while others used more moderate approaches. In Canada, there was continuity. Government programs tightened the funding available for social experimentation (Keck and Fulk, 1997), but organizing continued. In both countries, there was a growth of Marxist organizations, and many activists chose factories as their place of struggle.

Several important tendencies emerged from the New Left, often more quietly and with less drama than the revolutionary struggles. Let us now look at three examples of continuity: new populism/and urban activism, women's organizing and services, and social movements.

CONTINUITIES AND DEVELOPMENTS

Some activists who had worked on projects in the late 1960s turned their energies to more systematic community organizing practice. Although they brought with them some of the radicalism of the student movement, they had also developed a practice that was more systematic, understanding that the revolution was not around the

corner and that community organizing was a long-term commitment. Throughout the 1970s, many initiatives emerged at the local
level, including the organizing of disenfranchised groups in organizations such as the National Welfare Rights Organization (NWRO)
in the United States. As I described in Chapter 1, one of my first
grassroots experiences was helping to set up a chapter of that organization near Ann Arbor, Michigan. The work was door-to-door and
combined education about rights with advocacy and local leadership
development. Similar initiatives, such as GMAPCC, occurred in
Canada, but a national organization based on a local chapter structure was never put in place. The emphasis on supporting local leadership and on creating organizations that allowed direct participation
by poor people marked the continuity with the New Left program.
The goal was to build a movement of the poor. Although gains were
made, the welfare poor were too small a constituency to build the
kind of movement that could go beyond the specific issues, such as
welfare, that touched that group.

In the 1970s activists turned to neighbourhood organizing. The
goals of such "neo-Alinsky" organizing is described by Fisher (1994):

> to develop mass political organizations rooted in
> neighborhoods, grounded in local concerns, and
> focused on winning concrete gains. The goal was to
> advance social and economic democracy, empower
> people, and challenge power relations in and beyond
> the neighborhood. (p. 146)

It was assumed that this could be accomplished only with a "majoritar-
ian strategy" that would include low and moderate incomes.

In the United States, populist organizations were informed and
inspired by long traditions; those using these traditions argued for a
widening of democracy and power for the people (Evans and Boyte,
1992). For example, the Mid-West Academy was established by
Heather Booth, a former SDS activist, to train community organizers. Another initiative, ACORN (Association of Community
Organizations for Reform Now) is perhaps the longest lasting and

most significant of these organizations. It grew out of low-income neighbourhoods in Arkansas and now has chapters in many states. Its funding is based on membership subscriptions. Working on local, state, and some national issues, it focusses on winning issues and has been able to do what Alinsky failed to do—work beyond the local and build from the local to the state and national levels.

In Montreal, the institute with which I was affiliated during the years 1974 to 1978 had been organizing poor people, following a welfare rights model. Feeling they had reached the limits of this approach, organizers went through a period of reflection about strategy. There were a number of reasons why they thought that working with the welfare poor had reached a dead end. Those receiving welfare benefits were too small a group to have much social power; moreover, many who were working for low wages and those receiving unemployment benefits shared many of the same issues as those on welfare, and their participation would broaden the base. In addition, the organizers began to adhere to a traditional class analysis, as did many activists in Quebec at the time. Building working-class power was the objective. Local organizing was part of a wider movement for basic social change that included a trade union movement that had shifted to the left. The organizing was similar to the Alinsky model, modified by attempts to bring organizations from different neighbourhoods together on common issues. There was a concerted effort made to undertake political education, exposing the power relations in society as a whole. The times supported the organizers to move in that direction as a strong left current ran through community and popular organizations at that time.

Glenn Drover and I (1979) wrote an article reflecting on that practice. We were critical of the process of organization-building and maintenance that required both financial support from outside agencies and a professional cadre of organizers who had indirect control over the organizing processes. We raised the following questions: "Can these struggles lead to alternative visions, and a serious challenge to capitalist hegemony or will they be played out within the dominant framework of reform?" (p. 69). Perhaps we were asking too much of neighbourhood organizing; nonetheless, we proposed three directions that we thought would contribute to a more radical/socialist alternative. The points included a critique of organization, a need to examine the disruptive power of community organizations, and the building of local alternative organizations. The debate that ensued reflects the differences between the populist or neo-Alinsky perspective and a socialist perspective, as well as the tension between those two visions—reformist and Marxist.

The New Left began to fragment by the beginning of the 1970s, although some activists continued to follow the orientations of the earlier periods—an open radical stance, with influences from a variety of sources. The organizing work continued with neo-Alinsky populism, but with clear influences from the older left traditions, such as anarchism. Others became involved in Marxist groups following Trotskyist or Maoist teachings. The practice of the latter was to work in factories as a way to politicize and mobilize the working class . However, another shift was to have a longer term impact and shape the struggles that followed. New social movements, particularly the women's and ecology movements, in many ways reshaped social action, taking it out of the community base and finding new expressions for opposition. I will not attempt to cover all aspects of this subject area because it is too vast, but I will examine several dimensions that have contributed in substantial and innovative ways to community organizing practice.

The feminist movement was able to both effectively put New Left principles into practice and to build theories from the practice that would reinforce the work of the movement. The ideas that I will present do not necessarily represent the ideas of the whole movement, which is made up of many different groups and tendencies, categorized as liberal, radical, and socialist (Adamson et al., 1988). Liberal feminism focusses on equal opportunity for women through the reform of existing structures. Radical feminism, based on the biological differences between men and women, argues for a society based on female, life-supporting values including cooperation, challenges to hierarchy, and anti-militarism, thus building a women-centred culture and corresponding organizations. Socialist feminism locates women's oppression in the interaction of four elements:

gender, class, race, and sexual orientation. It links these dimensions to the economic structure and challenges the power based on them, while arguing for fundamental change. They go further in differentiating between strategies for change that are institutionalized and those that are grassroots. The former operates and works for change within the institutions of society, such as government and political parties, while the latter is community-based, involves collective organizing, reaches out to women "on the street," and works at consciousness-raising.

It is at the level of the grassroots that women introduced significant innovation in community organizing. One of the departures and important lessons for practice that followed was the understanding that one must look beyond traditional organizations and parliamentary processes as vehicles for social change. Rather, according to Adamson, Briskin, and McPhail (1988) social change can be promoted through "popular collective movements." They argue:

> Collective action is the extension of the belief in the collective. Collective action as a route to change empowers people in the face of their individual powerlessness. It encourages the active, ongoing participation of large numbers and the pooling of resources by marginalized groups usually excluded from formal political power, and validates both our right and our power to change not only ourselves, but the world around us ... participation on collective action is often the route to individual change. (p. 155)

One of feminism's central principles is that the personal cannot be separated from the political. Social struggle implies personal change, and personal change encourages social engagement. The joining of the public and private spheres was a big step forward. For example, the struggles around reproductive rights and domestic violence followed and contributed to the strengthening of this practice. In terms of the organizing process, Adamson et al. (1988) argue:

> the connection between personal problems and public
> solutions did more than direct women's attention
> towards the overall social change: it also helped to
> break down the numbing isolation of personal experi-
> ence and to activate women politically. (p. 201)

These lessons were vital for other identity-centred movements such as ones based on disability or sexual orientation. These move- ments grew in size as individuals who redefined personal oppression in political terms effectively encouraged others to feel safe to do the same. The organizing discussed earlier concerns a process in which one group—the organizers, the politicos—organizes others—usually the poor, the working class, etc. The women's movement and those that followed began with organizing on their own personal issues, seeing how these are shared by others in similar circumstances, and then trying to do something about it. The form of organizing also changed; organizers were part of the process. They were not outsiders who did not necessarily experience the issues first-hand. Because it was a social movement, practice went beyond single organizations; linkages between diverse types of organization and practice were forged in the struggle for common objectives. This created strength in terms of the capacity to mobilize and to educate people beyond the membership of a particular group. Participation was inclusive of many perspectives and practices. New organizations were put in place that carried forward the values and practices of the movement—the cre- ation of a democratic space and the solidarity between women.

However, like other social movements and groups, there are debates about strategy. Briskin (1991) summarizes two positions that emerged from within the women's movement—disengagement and mainstreaming. The former, she argues, "operates from a critique of the system and a standpoint outside of it, and a desire, therefore, to create alternative structures and ideologies." The latter "operates from a desire to reach out to the majority of the population with popular and practical feminist solutions to particular issues" (p. 30). She argues that the movement requires both and that each has its risks. "Disengagement can lead to marginalization and invisibility;

mainstreaming to co-optation and institutionalization" (p. 31). The creation of alternative institutions was and is a strong feature of the feminist movement. These include shelters for women subjected to violence, rape crisis centres, and a variety of community and collective projects that have brought women together. At the same time, campaigns for improving women's lives, such as the right to abortion, have led to important victories.

The tension discussed by Briskin is present in a variety of other places in the community movement. Groups try to create their own services and projects to create a place in which they have control and a defining voice. But, at the same time, they must question if the energy spent on these activities will isolate them and, perhaps more important, mitigate against their participation in wider mobilization and political engagement. The recent World March of Women 2000, as it was organized in Quebec, was highly successful precisely because the networks of service and local activity could be mobilized and brought together for a common cause.

The women's movement took the organization question further than the New Left and put into practice new forms of service provision. These challenged the dominant division between professional and client, and were managed through collective processes. Ristock (1991) describes the organizations as follows:

> Collective practices for the delivery of services, internal processes, and perceptions of work reflect a consistency between their organizational structure and feminist principles. Identifying hierarchical, bureaucratic organizations as perpetuating a power imbalance in our society, they remain committed to consensus decision-making practices. They have adopted the egalitarian principle that each worker is used according to her own strengths, and not according to educational background. (p. 43)

Ristock goes on to discuss some of the difficulties and contradictions that have been faced by feminist collectives. In spite of problems, these organizations create the possibility of democracy as part of everyday life and give people the opportunity to exercise some control over their work life. In addition, the practice has taken the initial impulse of the New Left into a realm where the conflicts between ideals and realities have to be confronted. It has succeeded in many instances in successfully building a tradition that combines a democratic form of organization with service provision and involvement with social struggles. I will examine some of the contradictions of these forms later in this book (see Chapter 4), but here I acknowledge the positive and innovative contributions of the women's movement and the links that it has with some of the ideas of the early New Left.

Other social movements also continued to develop the New Left's ideals and theories during the latter part of the twentieth century. There is a vast literature that analyzes these movements, but I will not explore that here. Rather, I want to describe some of the forms of action that have been developed. A tradition of direct action continues, influenced less by community organizing than by the peace and other social movements. Noël Sturgeon (1995) describes the use of nonviolent direct action tactics and working outside of mainstream institutions. Their identifying characteristics include the use of affinity groups, consensus forms of decision-making, and tactics that include direct confrontation and civil disobedience. Campaigns such as those against nuclear weapons and nuclear power, forms of discrimination, and globalization have been conducted through these forms of direct action. The affinity groups are a central aspect and remind me of the attempt of the community organizers from ERAP to build community for themselves as well as engaging in struggles for wider social change. Affinity groups, according to Sturgeon (1995):

> form a decentralized organizational structure that
> minimizes bureaucracy and formal leadership, consis-
> tent with the antihierarchical proclivities of the move-
> ment…. the members of the affinity group construct
> an obligation to each other that is based only on their
> participation in consensus process and their mutual
> political action. … [It] serves as a symbol of an alterna-

tive political order intended to be placed against the straight lines and hierarchical structures of police barricades and military facilities. (p. 39)

These social movements do not take the form of traditional organizations, but they may receive support from existing organizations as allies. They are based on the assumption that mass mobilization is the best expression of opposition, and opposition is best expressed through direct confrontations. The relationship between social movements and community organizing is symbiotic. Each contributes to the health of the other, but they are different. Social movements tend to have a period of growth, a decline, and then a rebirth. Community organizing tends to be encapsulated in an organizational form with specific mandates and staff. The principle of an organization is that it can overcome the unstable nature of social movements. However, as we discussed earlier, it is difficult to sustain the momentum of the more radical aspects of these organizations over time.

COMMUNITY ACTION: CONCLUDING COMMENTS

Let us return to the questions raised earlier in the chapter. First, what is the relationship of context to practice? What opportunities and constraints occur? The combination of a growing economy, an active interventionist government, a student/youth left, and other social movements, interacted in tension throughout the 1960s and 1970s. Governments in both the United States and Canada were in the midst of a period of social reform. In the United States, it was in response to the civil rights movement and urban unrest, while in Canada there was a strong trade union movement, a nationalist movement in Quebec with a left-wing orientation, and a strong, radical youth movement. Part of both governments' response was to "cool out" the more radical edge by drawing participation into their sanctioned programs and directing dissent toward established channels. In order to do this, at least in the beginning, there was flexible and decentralized funding for different types of activities. The double conditions that supported organizing were the social movements that provided the base, by contesting aspects of the wider society, and the government provision of money to direct these actions into "safer" directions. The results were opportunities to expand an action strategy. At the same time, this was a constraint. A reliance on state programs and money and the normal rise and fall of social movements were a weakness that resulted in the demise of some action organizing. However, there has been continuity in the ideas and practices of the earlier period to the social movements of today. Thus, even though the earlier period did not make the dramatic gains envisioned, its legacy and contributions were passed down the line to other activists and movements.

Two interrelated issues are the social vision and its contribution to practice and the processes of practice. There are different visions, and these did not always enter into the day-to-day activities of community organizations with any coherence. The organizers influenced by Alinsky and his followers believed that it was possible, within the political system, for citizens to represent their interests through organization-building coupled with pressure tactics. They believed in the openness of the state to accommodate, albeit reluctantly, the demands of these groups. In contrast, the New Left and the social movements that followed had an explicit critique of the system and, at least in theory, sought fundamental change. The problem was that effective practice was also defined by the winning of concessions. The tension, then, is between the vision and the practice, and the problem is to connect the two. There were a couple of ways that this occurred. First, the question of the form of organization was accorded central importance both in the organizing attempts of the New Left and in the social movements that followed. Organizing was about building a democratic community in which all members could have a voice. A community organization was to be a democratic space based on direct participation. Through challenging traditional notions of representative democracy and substituting more direct forms, organizers believed that the resulting social and political empowerment would spill over into other aspects of peoples' lives. This would, in turn, lead to other changes and processes both in public institutions and private lives.

In the course of organizing, what messages are conveyed to participants? The New Left and other social movements contributed to a critical social analysis while working for specific changes. Consciousness-raising, introduced by the women's movement, was designed to link personal experiences of oppression with a political understanding of wider relations of power and domination. This is diffuse but central and contributes to the creation of a culture of opposition. Community organizing can contribute to this through supporting and encouraging a critical analysis that links specific issues to political and social processes and the relations of power. Another important condition is forging connections to other similar organizations, campaigns, and social movements. In other words, community organizations cannot remain isolated but need to build solidarity with others. Without these links, community organizations can end up retreating into their own "backyards" and remain isolated.

If there is any conclusion that can be drawn, it is that there is no conclusion. Community action organizing from Alinsky to contemporary social movements shares similarities and differences. Organizing can work for all of the ideologies Fisher discussed from reactionary through to radical. The challenge for those struggling for progressive change is to understand how to use the tools and traditions that can contribute to their goals. The next chapter will examine how the community movement lost sight of its critical edge and became by its expertise and professionalism an extension of state-defined services and development.

CHAPTER FOUR

COMMUNITY DEVELOPMENT: COMMUNITY AS CONTAINMENT?

Community development has a long history in Canada and elsewhere. Its importance has shifted within the context of its practice. After a period in which it played second fiddle to social action in the relatively short period described in the previous chapter, it has made a comeback, once again becoming the dominant form of practice. Here, I will examine this practice and its underlying assumptions and beliefs. Following a brief historical perspective and definitions, I will analyze the links between the context and its development with an emphasis on the growth in importance of "civil society." Two practice approaches—asset-building and community economic development (CED)—that have emerged from this tradition will be examined in some depth. Finally, I will explore the question of the role and potential of this practice as a contributor to the process of social change as well as some of the tensions implicit in it.

The model that Rothman (1974) described as locality or community development has a long tradition, which Jim Lotz (1998) has traced. He presents many different practice examples ranging from land grant colleges in the United States in the early twentieth century that aimed to improve living conditions of rural communities, to attempts by French-speaking minorities in Nova Scotia to create cultural and economic institutions that would preserve their linguistic and cultural heritage. In addition, he discusses the role of community development in managing the British Empire in the 1930s. In 1955, the United Nations described community development, defining its central elements as follows:

> Community development can be tentatively defined as a process designed to create conditions of economic and social progress for the whole community with its active participation and the fullest reliance on the community's initiative. (United Nations, 1955, p. 6)

Some of the dominant values include: "democratic procedures, voluntary cooperation, self-help, development of indigenous leadership and education" (p. 4). Similarly, at a 1954 conference in Cambridge, England, community development was defined as: "A movement designed to promote better living for the whole community with the active participation and on the initiative of the whole community"(Lotz, 1998, p. 119). Lotz describes the community development workers as "an odd blend of idealists and realists, seeking better ways of meeting human needs than the societies offered the ordinary people of their time" (p. 125). Elsewhere, he writes that community workers would encourage "cooperation between all residents" and "self-help and local enterprise" (Lotz, 1997, p. 25). Lotz cites the beliefs of one Métis social worker, Jean Lagassé, as follows:

1. That all people, no matter how unambitious they may appear, have a desire to better themselves.
2. The difficulties preventing the fulfillment of people's needs are too great for the resources which they have.
3. All groups can do something to help themselves when given an opportunity to do so on their own terms.
4. In order to achieve lasting change it is necessary to influence simultaneously human behavior. (Lagassé, 1961, quoted in Lotz, 1998, p. 23)

Similar perspectives reappeared in the 1990s (see Kretzman and McKnight, 1993; Homan, 1999; and Ewalt et al., 1998). More recently, Frank and Smith (1999) proposed the following definition of community development:

> Community development is the planned evolution of all aspects of community well-being (economic, social, environmental and cultural). It is a process whereby community members come together to take collective action and generate solutions to common problems....The primary outcome of community development is improved quality of life. Effective community development results in mutual benefits and responsibility among community members. (p. 6)

Although there is a rhetoric of change, in contrast to the social or community action approach, this change is usually focussed inward on the community itself rather than outward on the wider social, economic, and political structures. Further, the process of working toward these changes is through consensus-building across interests rather than organizing to promote specific interests of the poor or oppressed groups. The emphasis is on meeting needs and finding pragmatic ways to do so in ways that do not challenge those with power. There is little discussion about inequality, interest, or power, or about the ways in which development can challenge these factors that play such a large role in shaping social issues and problems. Lotz (1998) raises questions about the role and impact of community development, observing: "In a paradoxical way, community development strives to stabilize society and encourage innovation and change in human relationships" (p. 26). This perspective stands in clear contrast to the action approach, which begins with an analysis of power and how it operates and promotes organizing as a tool for those without power to strengthen their collective voices. Community development believes in democratic participation by people to find solutions to issues and problems, but this is done within boundaries shaped by power relations already in place. I don't want to write off community development as irrelevant for the process of social change. It does offer opportunities for building democratic practices and creating ways that people can learn to take greater control of their own lives. However, the dominant practice has reinforced the overriding power relations and social values of society rather than challenging them.

SOCIAL CAPITAL AND CIVIL SOCIETY

In analyzing the shift in community practice from social activism to development, context is an important factor. From the 1980s onward responsibility for social provision has shifted from the welfare state to a combination of the market (privatization), the family, and organizations in local communities. The concepts of "social capital" and "civil society" have emerged in a significant way as social policy options coincident with the rise of globalization, economic restructuring, and cutbacks. In response to this restructuring, the state and other social actors attribute greater importance to the community sector as the source of social provision through the community development model. Given the extensive debates and literatures around the concepts of social capital and civil society, I shall present brief definitions of each and then raise questions about how they have shaped the development model in the current context.

Homan (1999) states:

> Social capital refers to community wealth derived from active engagement of individuals with other members of the community.... These engagements provide opportunities for affiliation among members and benefits to the community. (p. 31)

Clarke and Gaile (1998) argue that both social and human capital provide important resources that contribute towards national economic competitiveness and the restructuring of local citizenship. For example, in order for cities to achieve economic success, both human capital—an educated workforce—and social capital—a local infrastructure—are necessary. However, despite the good reasons for tying resources to social capital, some writers have been concerned about the difficulty in creating and sustaining it. This position is put forward in Putnam's important article "Bowling Alone: America's Declining Social Capital" (1995). He offers many reasons for this decline, including the entry of women into the labour market, the decline of the trade union movement, and the growth of privatized forms of entertainment. McKnight (1995B) attributes the reduction of social capital to the dominant role played by professionals in many aspects of social life. So here is the problem: social capital is necessary to enhance daily life, but it is declining and difficult to re-establish. Putnam (1995) concludes that in order to counter this trend, the public agenda should add "the question of how to reverse these adverse trends in social connectedness, thus restoring civic engagement and civic trust" (p. 77). With the retreat of government and the fragmentation of neighbourhoods as social units, the renewal of community development surfaces as a strategy to restore local social practices to fill the void. At the same time, this practice does not challenge the underlying causes of the problems.

A similar line of argument can be seen in the promotion of civil society. Sheri Torjman, in *Civil Society: Reclaiming Our Humanity* (1997), a document written for the Caledon Institute of Social Policy, promotes the growth and development of civil society, which, she says:

> sustains and enhances the capacity of all its members
> to build a caring and mutually responsible society ...
> all citizens—individual, corporate and government—
> assume responsibility for promoting economic, social
> and environmental well-being. (p. 2)

Civil society seeks to achieve three major objectives: caring communities, economic security, and social investment. All sectors, including governments, business, labour, education, foundations, and social agencies, must take responsibility for tackling economic, social, and environmental issues, working collaboratively and addressing issues in a holistic and integrated way (Torjman, 1997, p. 2). Active citizenship implies building caring communities that embody both rights and responsibilities.

The first ingredient in a civil society is capital, including finance, natural/built, and human. Finance capital ranges from community loan funds, where control of capital is in the hands of community-based organizations; credit unions, which support micro-business; and private-sector corporations and/or foundations that support some types of community initiatives. Natural/built capital refers to use of space including land and buildings in such diverse ownership practices as land trusts and shopping malls. Human capital is defined as "the wealth inherent in human resources" (Torjman, 1997, p. 11), based on the capacities of all to contribute and the mobilization of these capacities through voluntary efforts.

Partnerships are the second ingredient of civil society and are defined as "strategic alliances between business and non-profit groups for the purpose of promoting economic and social well-being" (Torjman, 1997, p. 12). Partnerships, including social mar-keting—that is, the use of the private sector to promote the work of community organizations—and employee voluntarism in commu-nity projects that work toward social and economic change, are deemed important because they raise awareness of social problems and create more resources to deal with them. At the same time, Torjman argues that partnerships complement and supplement the public sector, embodying the message that economic, social, and environmental issues are the concerns of the whole community. Thus, the call for a renewal of civil society is shaped by the need to reconstruct community as a place of service and support, a place in which all interests can come together for the benefit of all.

There are common elements in the promotion of civil society and social capital and the practice of CED and the community develop-ment model. These concepts are based on the assumption that society is shaped by the common concern of all rather than conflicts of inter-est and that the means to achieve good ends is through social and eco-nomic partnerships. Because interest and partnership are key issues that differentiate the community action from the development models, I would like to raise a couple of critical issues. Torjman's analysis implies that all members of society share a common stake and responsibility. This position is politically dangerous, because it overlooks questions of interest and power. Citizens, corporations, and government have never shared common interests. To announce a new "caring, mutually responsible society" is to wipe the historical slate clean and to ignore the fact that underlying interests remain. Similarly, to start with the category of "individual/citizen" assumes a commonality that is not borne out in history. The implicit precept is that a common interest exists—that all of us want to walk into the "promised land" hand-in-hand. Yet, class, gender, race, and location in the world all determine how social life is defined. Thus, historical discontinuity becomes coupled with political naiveté.

The argument that all sectors must take responsibility for social well-being is fine in the most general terms, but history shows us that it is precisely because capital and the state have not assumed their responsibility for social provision that social struggles have ensued and continue to aim at extracting social gains. Why were (and are) these struggles necessary? Primarily, capital—first locally, then nationally, and now globally—is not self-regulating; the only limits to its power has been state intervention through legislation such as minimum wage and welfare state programs. There has never been anything approaching "equal responsibility"; capital has no vested interest in place or people. Those who control it can and will do whatever is necessary in the push for profit. At best, Torjman's approach will result in tinkering with the consequences of economic restructuring and state cutbacks through the provision of unstable local services and a few programs. A more effective plan is to focus on the root of the problems and to identify the alliances necessary to challenge basic power relations.

New community developers assume that partnerships between different groups in society are an integral aspect of social change. Many issues arise from this position. First, partnerships are real when they are established between different groups within a common project in which the goals and values are clearly defined. This implies a process of discussion and debate between partners and a consensus with movement on all sides. This is quite different than a partnership in which one group—the corporate sector to use the example cited in

Torjman's document—drops in and does something for or with the community sector. The former implies a common project with power sharing among the different participants, while the latter is an extension of a charity relation under a different label.

The question, however, concerns what kinds of compromises are made by the community sector when entering into partnerships with socially and economically stronger partners. Who has the power, and what interests are being served? Why is it that the corporate sector is willing to enter into partnerships when it comes to social intervention, but does not ask the community sector into partnership when it comes to questions of corporate policy? For example, corporations make policies such as downsizing or shifting investment elsewhere that have major impacts on the local community; yet, local community organizations are not invited to share in this process. The community sector can organize food banks for the unemployed and may receive some corporate donations towards that goal, but where is the real public accountability of those entities motivated by private profit to close down factories? Until the relationship is truly reciprocal, the partnership association will be skewed to one side, with the community sector as a very small player.

Partnerships are the current currency of community development. They pull community organizations into relationships that hide power and interest. I am not implying that community organizations should not enter into these relationships, but they should do so only if they recognize the interests involved and have the power to co-define the relationship.

The promotion of these definitions of civil society and social/human capital as a direction for the community movement raises a number of difficulties. Their underlying assumption obscures their basic premise—in order to contribute to the process of social change, community organizations have to understand society from the viewpoint of the interests of their government and corporate partners, not the specific interests of groups such as the poor, women, and many minorities, who face barriers not because of who they are but because of social policies and processes. The demands and struggles for social justice must be the central agenda for community organizations. Having argued this, can notions of civil society be useful? The use of this term is loose and, as such, is too inclusive and lacks a conceptual framework. For instance, it has been used to refer to a number of popular, non-governmental organizations (NGOs) which have been involved in protests against free trade, globalization, and greater corporate power. The contradiction is evident when organizations positioned on opposite sides of the globalization debate (for instance) use the same term—civil society—to describe themselves. Some organizations, like the community economic development corporations discussed later in this chapter, actively participate in a new social consensus and work toward responses to deteriorating social and economic conditions that do not challenge those with power, while others, such as the anti-corporate globalization groups, are active in their opposition to the prevailing economic and social arrangements. Some organizations can live in both places, providing new services and then mobilizing for demonstrations. Jamie Swift (1999) captures this tension:

> The concerns of civil society ... are clearly not the concerns of unfettered market forces that generate social disintegration and inequality. This thing called civil society, then, has a role in the protection of the public good, even if, again, it cannot automatically be assumed to be a Good Thing ... or looked on as a neo-liberal substitute for the state.... These projects [services] are fine, but do little by themselves to enable people ... to take more control over the decisions that have an impact on their lives ... we can locate civil society as a space, separate from formal politics but very much politically engaged, where people act on issues that impinge on them directly or where they promote a more general public good. (p. 147)

Thus, we see that the term has a dual meaning and suggests possibility for change. Civil society can be described as a space that is neither occupied by the economy nor the state, but is not necessarily independent of them. Within this space, a variety of activities is possible, ranging from protest to conventional charity. At the same time, the building of civil society has been promoted and supported as a way to replace state services and build a stifling social consensus and partnership. Knowing the difference is the beginning of a politics of social change.

ASSETS AND CAPACITY

Within the context of civil society, community development has taken on an important role. A major proponent of this renewal is John McKnight. He has written extensively about community development, and consulted widely with a large number of organizations and people with power to influence community practice. His work is complex and combines both a radical and a conservative vision. His radicalism comes in the form of a fundamental challenge to the power of professionals, particularly those who work in the community, such as social workers, and the so-called "helping" professions (doctors, nurses, etc). He defines one of the most significant problems facing the United States as the growing control of all aspects of daily life by those professions, which, as a consequence, have eclipsed the democratic life of the community. He writes:

> It is clear that the economic pressure to professional-
> ize requires an expanding universe of need and the
> magnification of deficiency. This form of marginal
> professional development can only intensify the inef-
> fective, dominating, and iatrogenic nature of the pro-
> fessional class as they invade the remaining perime-
> ters of personhood. (McKnight, 1995B, pp. 23–24)

His task is to find a way to "dissolve the 'professional problem'" (p. 25). The perspective he constructs for the relationship between the professions and those they are "helping" is based on citizenship—as opposed to client—and assets—as opposed to deficiencies. He argues for a practice that strengthens the capacity of people to control and manage their lives through a vibrant and democratic community.

However, the radical veneer can be peeled off the surface to reveal the conservative core: for McKnight, community is understood as a relatively self-contained unit, and change is an inward-looking process.

Kretzman and McKnight (1993) put their practice orientation into a broad context, maintaining that the crisis of work has had devastating consequences for low-income communities, removing the "bottom rung from the fabled American 'ladder of opportunity'" (p. 1). They argue that the solution cannot be found by focussing on deficiencies and problems, which is the way that these problems are usually approached. These types of intervention usually command most of the resources. They offer a different starting point—a clear commitment to a community's capacities and assets. The traditional practice is to point out problems and then to construct services as a solution to them, thus creating a dependency that reduces people from their potential status as citizens to clients with a reliance on outside experts. This "needs based strategy can guarantee only survival and can never lead to serious change or community development ... this orientation must be replaced as one of the major causes of the sense of hopelessness that pervades discussion about the future of low-income communities" (p. 5). McKnight and Kretzman propose an alternative that they call "capacity focussed development." Significant community development can only take place when local people commit themselves to investing their resources and efforts, thus avoiding a top-down or an outside-in practice, although the prospect for outside help is bleak because of budgetary constraints and weak job prospects. The basic goal, then, is to mobilize assets to build community involving "virtually the entire community in the complex process of regeneration" (p. 345). The solution to the professional service problem is to use existing assets within the community to create networks of self-help and support. McKnight and Kretzman (1999) believe that "identifying the variety and richness of skills, talents, knowledge of people in low-income neighborhoods provides a base upon which to build new approaches and enterprises" (p. 160). However, they recognize some of the limits of what can be achieved locally and argue that low-income neighbourhoods should "develop their assets and become interdependent with mainstream people, groups and economic activity" (p. 171).

McKnight's disciples disregard the radical challenges he puts forward, concentrating instead on those parts that fit nicely into an acceptable practice for the neo-liberal 1990s and then professionalizing it. For example, Homan (1999) presents a summary of the elements of practice that follow from this perspective. The starting point is the recognition that the existing assets of a community are those factors that give it energy to take action. Teaching individuals a variety of skills builds on their capacities. Connecting people and building relationships between them allows individuals to share their talents through linkages with existing community resources. Homan states: "Whenever you connect resources, you create investors.... You extend ownership and participation" (p. 37). The next step is to create or increase community resources—to bring something new into existence. A pillar of this process is community ownership of the direction, actions, and resources; in other words, the community creates the plans, not just approves them. The expectation is that the members of the community will do all the work. At the same time as internal capacity is built up, beneficial external relations are necessary, and so alliances are made with other communities and sources of public support. The fundamental goal is to foster community self-reliance and confidence. This can be achieved through self-sustaining organizations, which provide effective mechanisms for community decision-making and a renewal of leadership. These steps are intended to enhance the general quality of life. The question of who will support these initiatives and provide the resources for them is ignored, including the dicey relationship between local organizations and those who fund them.

Comprehensive Community Initiatives (CCI) provides another example of the new community development in practice. Ewalt (1998) argues that CCI goes beyond sectoral practices and is an example of a "multifaceted approach that addresses the physical and economic conditions of a neighborhood as well as the social and cultural aspects" (p. 3). These initiatives are based on community partnership or some form of local governance with citizen participation in decision-making. Naparstek and Dooley (1998) discuss a community-building approach that

> looks at the whole picture, acknowledges the inter-
> connectedness of people- and place-based strategies,
> and recommends a course of action in which solu-
> tions are tied together in such a way that they rein-
> force one another ... that will give neighborhood res-
> idents more control over changes and the ability to
> hold accountable the larger systems that ought to be
> serving them. (p. 11)

In 1993, the United States government created the Empowerment
Zone program, designed to support neighbourhood development and
alleviate poverty. The program has four elements: a geographically
defined target, strategic planning based on a definition of community,
community participation in the governance of the program, and comprehensive—economic, physical, and human—development (Chaskin,
Joseph, and Chipenda-Dansokho, 1998). The push for a focus on the
local occurs in a context in which the wider social programs that might
have had an major impact—wide-scale construction of social housing,
adequate income support, federal health care, or initiatives to regulate
economic development—have disappeared from the national agenda.
In their place, the community is given responsibility to revitalize itself
with programs controlled from the outside, although administered
locally. Thus, the internal process of community development
becomes the vehicle for the implementation of a "de-responsibilized"
national government, and local democratic processes act, perhaps
unintentionally, to legitimate these changes.

The positive contributions of this approach come from the older
traditions of community development that emphasize process and
participation of citizens and that insist on local control of community
processes with citizens playing an active role in building community
projects. The idea of people having power to control local institutions and processes is a necessary first step. But a step towards what?
This question is at the heart of the differences between com-
munity/social action and development. McKnight (1995B) clarify this
difference by arguing:

> Organizations originally oriented to the goal of equal-
> izing consumption patterns between and within
> neighborhoods are increasingly turning toward an
> agenda that centers on building internal neighbor-
> hood productive capacities. (p. 157)

In other words, do not look outside for help, for redistribution of wealth and income, but fulfill your own needs through mobilizing local resources. This is the "bootstrap" theory of poverty reduction: if the poor work hard and prepare themselves adequately, then they, too, can succeed within capitalist society. Thus, the critique of this approach is that it focusses on changing internal community processes while ignoring both the underlying assumptions about why this should be done and the conservative political agenda that it implicitly supports.

McKnight's approach contributed to the acceptance of community development as mainstream by governments, foundations, and those in practice, as well as by researchers and writers in the field. The time was ripe for this new direction. With the deterioration of social and economic conditions in the mid-1970s, ideological attacks from the right challenged both social gains made through the welfare state and the legitimacy of the state's social role. Budget cuts on the social side were the order of the day, with those at the bottom bearing the burden of fiscal conservatism. One of the consequences, for example, was that rather than attacking poverty, governments launched offensives against the poor themselves, not only by removing programs and benefits but also by questioning basic entitlement to these programs. Economic changes parallelled the redefinition of the role of the state. Unions were put on the defensive as employers sought a more "flexible" workplace to enable greater competition in global markets. This combined with accelerating technological innovation to bring massive unemployment in the 1980s and much of the 1990s. The new jobs that replaced traditional blue-collar work were neither unionized nor stable. Even with the reduction in unemployment in the late 1990s, poverty was not diminished because, for many, work became more precarious and irregular. With the collapse of the Soviet

Union, the world has entered a period of global capitalism, in which markets rule, and the bottom line is on top. There is a deeply rooted feeling of inevitability that possibilities for progressive social change no longer exist, and there seems to be little hope for those with a progressive social vision. The traditional social democratic parties in Canada and the Democratic Party in the United States, when in power, have all abandoned their social commitments and supported the corporate agenda.

How does community organizing practice fit with all these changes? At first, activists in the community sector opposed the cutbacks in government spending on services and programs. As the years passed, it became clear that neo-liberalism was gaining rather than losing ground, and, as the new economy emerged from the restructuring, it appeared that a return to postwar employment patterns and the welfare state was unlikely. Community organizations and organizers faced a dismal situation. There was little energy to continue the kind of social action struggles that dominated the 1960s and 1970s, and poverty and unemployment, coupled with the reduction in social programs, drove large numbers of new clients to community-based organizations and services to seek help. The community sector responded by providing new forms of social support and creating ways to build local solidarity through programs like food banks, which became a growth industry in the 1980s and a permanent part of the landscape by the 1990s. However, such programs have lost their political edge.

Pushed by the new economic and political realities, the community organizations looked for wider strategies to combat the social and economic problems they faced. The "shift" that McKnight and Kretzmann identified describes the repositioning of community organizations from an oppositional to a collaborative stance, from seeking confrontation and challenging the power structure to finding common ground and building a new social consensus with it. Further, both governments and private foundations have embraced this new community development practice, partly because community organizations have cushioned the blows to the lives of the poor and the working class, while asking for very little from the state in their attempts to go beyond service provision to promote local revitalization strategies.

Some of the limits of the new community development practices and approaches have been explored by various critics. For instance, McGrath, Moffat, and George (1999) have criticized McKnight and the community development practices that have sprung from his work. First, they say that the discussion of community capacity building is ahistorical, ignoring such rich traditions as popular education and feminism. McKnight's assumption concerning the necessity of building local capacity is not new but has been used before, often with a vision of fundamental social change. Second, they argue that community development assumes the availability of voluntary labour as the basis for releasing the unused capacity within communities. However, the growth of women's employment in wage labour and the demands on them for caregiving in the home because of state cutbacks of services have diminished their voluntary contribution, even if that kind of volunteer activity were desirable. Thus, the model may be more applicable in wealthier communities where (perhaps) women are freer to volunteer their labour. Third, as opposed to McKnight who assumes a coherence in local communities, McGrath et al. state that communities are fragmented by identity and interest and that one cannot necessarily find either unity or common ties within them. Finally, they challenge McKnight's belief that the community sector is independent of the state. In contrast, they point out how organizations and their processes have been shaped by the changes in the welfare state both through funding and the definition of their activities.

Another problem associated with an increased emphasis on community development is that the local community has very limited power to shape its internal processes. In contrast, David Morris (1996) promotes the idea that "[a]uthority, responsibility, and capacity are the cornerstones of sustainable communities" (p. 437). Authority implies the mandate to make rules to protect and enhance community life and raises the dimension of decentralized power, which can be used formally by those at the local level to effect real change by having control over processes, such as zoning or economic planning. Building capacity without political power is a dead end. In addition, capacity brings the power and confidence that comes with ownership of economic tools. As Morris states:

> Authority, responsibility, capacity: the ARC of com-
> munity. Without authority, democracy is meaningless.
> Without responsibility, chaos ensues. Without pro-
> ductive capacity, we are helpless to manage our affairs
> and determine our economic future. (p. 445)

The concept of capacity-building and the related process of community development are not the problem; it is the context in which they are practices that is key. If capacity-building and community development are used to build local power and authority, to represent the interests of low-income populations, and to struggle for social justice, then they can contribute to a social change strategy. If their goal is to make limited changes in community life, as an end in itself and as a way of creating networks of "helpful citizens," then the outcome will support the neo-liberal policies we have seen imposed in recent years.

COMMUNITY ECONOMIC DEVELOPMENT (CED)

CED is a strategy that has been developed primarily but not exclusively in response to the deterioration of local economies and the lack of hope for revitalization from the outside, either from the private market through investment or with the support of government programs. Initiatives that featured leadership from community organizations and partnership relations with local actors, such as the private sector, unions, local institutions, and government, were designed to create new economic options to provide jobs, services, or infrastructure. Through these processes, community organizations have now become players in the process of economic development (Shragge, 1997). Practices have varied from the promotion of small-scale enterprises that employ people who face long-term unemployment, to loan funds to support CED initiatives, to planning initiatives that promote local economic development. The underlying goals are to find ways to revitalize local economies, ameliorate poverty through training and job creation, and to involve residents and other local actors in these processes. What led to these changes have been the conditions of unemployment, low-wage precarious jobs, and poverty, at a time when government social services were diminishing.

The new practices include economic initiatives such as skills training and job creation programs. Social solidarity, as well as the recognition that the state has abandoned its responsibility and is unlikely to resume its role as the central provider, has motivated the emphasis on economic development and related services. Further, a new strategy of consensus-based partnerships has created alliances of community organizations, business, government, and, at times, unions (particularly in Quebec) to sponsor new local initiatives. These have been directed toward finding limited solutions to problems without examining their causes. They have obscured conflicting interests and differentials in power. The community sector, as the politically weakest player, does the front-line work of implementing programs defined from the outside by government and foundations. The problem then becomes how local organizations can maintain enough autonomy to define and put in place activities that reflect neighbourhood priorities. The differences between initiatives reflect the strength of local groups and their traditions and their own approaches to CED practice.

Differing definitions of CED reflect differences in fundamental analyses and values. Michael Swack (1992) argues that the premise of CED is the strengthening of local capacity to mobilize resources and to use these to build a strong economic base for the community. CED seeks to change the economic structure of the community and to build permanent economic institutions, thus achieving greater control over local resources. It is a people-initiated strategy, which seeks to develop the economy of the community, region, or country for the benefit of its residents. CED is a systematic and planned intervention intended to promote economic self-reliance. One of its principal objectives is to help consumers to become producers, users to become providers, and employees to become owners of enterprises. CED does not assume that the market alone will solve the communities' economic problems. It utilizes entrepreneurship methods similar to those used by traditional businesses in the private sector to develop efficient productive and profitable ventures and enterprises, but does so in the context of a community's social, cultural, and political values. Swack's definition is fundamental and looks at the potential of local initiatives to use economic development as a tool to achieve social ends.

Another approach comes from De Roche (1998) who, drawing on Fontan's (1993) definitions, differentiates between "liberal" and "progressive" CED. The liberal tradition is economic development for and by the community. It does not challenge basic economic relations, but is business development from the bottom up. It aims to repair the economic fabric of the private sector in order to create jobs. Local revitalization can take place through the promotion of private entrepreneurship and related measures to develop the "employability" of the population and the creation of related jobs. In contrast, the progressive vision is broader and places greater emphasis on social processes. Thus, the progressive tradition attempts to integrate economic and social development; to improve the community's environment and quality of services; to build local control over ownership; and to create alternative non-traditional economic forms such as cooperatives, alternative businesses, community enterprises, self-management, and non-profit companies.

Bruyn (1987) and Roseland (1998) have developed progressive orientations. Bruyn argues that, historically, we have been presented with a false choice between "a free market with electoral democracy" and an undemocratic, restrictive, interventionist state with central planning (state socialism). He argues for a third option in which the role of the state is not to regulate the economy but to enable it to regulate itself and become accountable to the people it affects. In order to overcome the problem of the market destroying the community without government control, the social emancipation of land, labour, and capital from the competitive market is a required step in the process leading to local autonomy. He argues that this transition can take place within the context of economic viability at the local level. Bruyn and his colleagues, in a book titled *Beyond the State and the Market*, demonstrate the viability of this strategy of transformation. They cite examples of how land, labour, and capital have been reinvented through local action. For example, community land trusts are a way of creating local ownership of land and keeping it out of the market. Worker cooperatives have a long tradition and are a tool that labour can use to own the means of production. Finally, community loan associations or credit unions manage capital democratically for local use. These alternatives created within the existing system use economic tools within a democratic framework for social objectives.

Roseland (1998) provides a perspective that merges the principles and goals of CED and "green," or ecologically sound, businesses in order to move toward what he calls "sustainable communities" (p. 160). Self-reliance implies that the community enhances its wealth through the development of its own resources. Tools to achieve this include maximizing the use of existing resources, circulating money within the community, reducing imports of goods and services, and creating new products. He also emphasizes the use of incentives to attract environmentally responsible businesses. Roseland argues that self-reliance does not imply the absence of support from outside bodies including government, and he advocates the use of lobbying for policies that can support the institutions and conditions for this green CED vision. This last point is particularly important because it raises the political dimension and the necessity of outside support in order to create the conditions to support local work.

There are many types of practice in either the liberal or progressive traditions that can be considered CED, but the factor that differentiates it from other community development practices is its economic or business component. Some CED practice is highly institutionalized through para-governmental organizations, such as those in Montreal that I discussed in Chapter 1. Beginning as local initiatives in working-class neighbourhoods in the mid-1980s, coalitions of labour, community organizations, and business sought strategies to combat poverty and unemployment resulting from economic deterioration and factory closures. Revitalization strategies—to save or restructure local business, to create new ones, or to establish training programs in order to get people back into employment—were to be put in place through local organizations. In addition, the structures of these organizations were to involve the local population through representation of different sectors on their boards. After the

development of three of these organizations, joint efforts by the
municipal, provincial, and federal governments resulted in the establishment of CED organizations in each of the city's administrative
districts with the exception of the downtown core. The programs of
these organizations were designed to provide technical and financial
support to both traditional and community businesses and to enhance
local residents' entry into the labour market. With subsequent
reforms in the late 1990s, these organizations have been integrated
into the provincial government network of development agencies.
With each reform, the autonomy of the organizations has become
diminished and their programs narrowed. There is some opportunity
for innovation and support for socially oriented community initiatives, such as day care and services for the elderly, as well as for projects such as eco-tourism. The advantages of these highly institutionalized CED organizations are their stability and the resources that
they offer, both technical and financial. The disadvantage is that, as
they have come under the control of the provincial government, the
local population has less power to shape their priorities and directions. In addition, as they have become part of the mainstream, their
activities focus much more on traditional, market-oriented business
development. The explicitly social aspects have become less pro-
nounced. An important struggle within these organizations has been
how to use their staff and other resources to provide assistance in
finding innovative solutions that go beyond the liberal perspective.

In contrast to institutionalized CED, there are independent organizations that use a CED strategy to reach social ends. Chic Resto-Pop
described in Chapter 2 is one such example. Another is A-Way Express
in Toronto (see Church, 1997). Founded by survivors of the mental
health system, it is a courier service whose employees use public trans-
portation to deliver letters, etc. However, in addition to its success as
a business, it is far more than that. A-Way describes itself as an alternative business. It was established partially to counter the myth that
people who have been institutionalized can never work and to build a
community of solidarity for this group. It provides a flexible work environment in which people can negotiate their hours based on their specific needs and capacities. In addition, it is democratically structured;

its leadership and the majority of its board of directors is drawn from employees, who are psychiatric survivors. At the same time as A-Way is using a business to reach social ends, it has resisted the idea that the business has to be "self-sustaining." It has successfully negotiated support from different outside bodies on a regular and ongoing basis. This support is justified on the social merits and outcomes of the business. Just as the private sector receives many different subsidies, grants, and supports from the government (often the bigger the business the bigger the support), it is an error to assume that CED initiatives must sustain themselves on their market-generated revenues. CED is a form of social development that uses business as a tool to achieve its goals. In the context of government cutbacks, organizations like A-Way play a significant social role, going beyond anything that the state can provide as an effective social service. Its strength is in its democratic practices and as a centre for personal and collective learning and power for a group that has been traditionally without voice. A-Way is just one example of an autonomous organization formed as a CED project to obtain social ends; there are many others.

PROBLEMS AND LIMITS OF CED

Some CED organizations have played a role in organizing a strong voice at the local level through which those without economic power can participate in shaping local economic development or creating democratic work places. However, the mainstream of CED is oriented toward much more traditional forms of business development determined by marketplace demands for profitability. Also, as economic power has become concentrated supra-nationally, the local has very little power in controlling its economic direction; investment is determined by those with little regard for the consequences of their choices on local life. CED thus faces the same dilemma as most organizing: it can create innovative alternatives and possibilities, and can open democratic spaces, but it has difficulty moving beyond the limits of government policy and market demands. The concerns that I raise grow out of doubts and personal questioning about my own involvement in CED practice. I feel that CED has some potential as a vehicle for social change and a means of building a voice for those excluded from economic debates in our society. But more often I see CED as a means of directing the community sector into an entrepreneurial mode without any vision of what can be gained by that process and without asking how business development can be a tool for social change.

In addition, CED is seen to a large extent as a strategy to reduce poverty, as a form of economic development that can provide low-income people with a way to participate in the capitalist economy. However, it is ironic that one of the reasons for the increase in poverty is the withdrawal of state intervention in regulating the market, while the state and others (e.g., foundations) have called upon poor communities to use the same less regulated market as a means of ameliorating local economic and social conditions. In other words, the state has lessened its responsibilities to deal with the social consequences of capitalism and its related social inequalities, while the poor themselves are told to step up and become entrepreneurs within the capitalist system that has failed to meet even their most basic employment need—a decent job with an adequate income. Can CED and associated small business do anything to ameliorate poverty without other extensive policies designed to redistribute income and wealth? Can they support in a large way alternative economic development and intervention in the private sector to limit exploitation? The danger of CED is that it is understood as a way for poor people to participate in and use the market economy rather than as a way of organizing on the local level for power to influence state policy to create democratic options. In an economic climate in which many new jobs tend to be low wage or in the service sector, does CED act to reproduce the same type of dead-end work that is being created elsewhere?

These questions plague CED practitioners. CED-related businesses and projects tend to pay very low wages or, as in the case of both A-Way and Resto-Pop, they benefit from the labour of those receiving social assistance. There are limited choices. Often the work in these businesses is far more desirable for the employees than no work at all, yet the issue of working conditions needs to be raised Another question involves the relationship between government and CED: as government has reduced spending on social programs, do CED practices that provide services act as a cheap replacement for government programs? For example, in recent years in Quebec there has been an increased demand for home care services for a variety of groups. Traditionally, these services have been provided by government clinics, in which the workers are unionized and have relatively permanent jobs as well as benefits. Home care services have shifted to the community sector, in CED projects offering low pay, no security, and no benefits as part of the new "social economy" (Shragge and Fontan, 2000). Thus, CED projects supported by government funding have created services that are far cheaper to operate and have little long-term commitment. It is important to understand how CED practices can be used by the state for its own purposes. Perhaps not all CED activities play this kind of role, but this example reminds us of the contradictions of practice and how it can be used to achieve different ends.

CED projects have to confront the power of the market in determining their success and sustainability. Without a strong commitment to democratic processes, mobilization, and popular education, CED can result in the "commodification" of social development. In other words, it represents a shift from what was once considered non-market processes—public services including local development—into goods and services to be bought and sold. The early vision of the welfare state was to take essential goods such as health care and education out of the market and treat them as basic social rights. With the shift to the community sector and some of the CED strategies, there is a tendency to create business out of what used to be considered public service. There is real pressure from the government's neo-liberal policy agenda to push CED practice in this direction. However, many of the diverse organizations involved in CED bring a rich tradition of opposition to this new context, and they have not been entirely swallowed up. Examples of this type of organizations include Chic Resto-Pop and A-Way organizations that have played a role in organizing a strong voice at the local level, a voice that can participate in shaping economic development and creating democratic work places. However, the CED mainstream is oriented toward much more traditional forms of business development determined by marketplace demands for profitability.

THE COMMUNITY DEVELOPMENT TRADITION: WORKING WITH THE CONTRADICTIONS

I have reviewed several ways in which the new community development is played out in practice. I have pointed out that the underlying belief of this approach is in social consensus, which obscures basic questions of interest and power. Its prominence is not really surprising given how the wider social and economic context has shaped current social problems and the possibilities of state response. Through the past 15 years of globalization and economic restructuring, the poor and the working class have been hit hard. The prospects of change seem minimal, and the options faced by the community sector limited. Government programs have been cut and in many instances pushed into the voluntary sector to be absorbed on the cheap by overly busy community organizations. Until the recent mobilizations against global free trade, opposition movements have been weakened and ignored by the arrogance of those promoting the corporate agenda. Trade unions, one traditional source of opposition, have seen their membership decline with the shift of traditional jobs away from Canada and the United States to the Third World and the growth of irregular work. Survival is the mode for many unions and community organizations. The latter are faced with growing demands for services to meet more complex and difficult social problems, and they have to do this with unstable funding. The new community development practices provide a way out. They legitimate the role of community organizations, but government and, at times, corporately backed foundations make sure that their social change objectives remains subservient to these services. Governments have used their new collaborative relations with community organizations as a way to organize social provision and economic development and to create the conditions to maintain harmony in a time of social deterioration. This is the bad news. I have deliberately overstated it, in order to emphasize the pressures on community organizations to adapt to the new realities.

However, there are also opportunities. Community organizations, despite the models and practices they have adopted or been pressured to adopt, carry a legacy of opposition and contestation. Examples from

Quebec include resistance to cutbacks and demands for better social housing, better social assistance, drug insurance programs, etc. These have all been led by coalitions of community organizations. For example, in fall 2000, an impressive mobilization for the World March of Women drew more than 20,000 into the streets of Montreal. Many community-based organizations and services mobilized their clients, staff, members, and boards to participate. This legacy of social action and the struggle for social justice co-exist with the development model in a complex tension. Push still comes from the radical, explicitly oppositional legacy, while the government and other sources of funding pull in a direction that neutralizes and professionalizes community organizations and uses them as cheap, flexible forms of social provision.

Despite my critique, I do not to write off the practice of community development. These organizations and processes bring together people who share common issues and problems. They can become a context for practices that may not be the primary function of the organization, but that can contribute to social change. Describing the context in which political space can be built, Barker (1999) uses the concept of an "activity centre" that:

> consists of a person or a set of people at a place and time engaged in a program of activity along with the objects and environmental features to which the activity is coordinated.... They are units in which individual and collective intention and creativity abound.... Each activity setting is a process of activity that exerts forces on people within the setting. Activity settings are structured contexts of forces most immediately surrounding persons and their activities." (pp. 30, 51)

Thus, activity centres create a place of local politics where a variety of outcomes are possible. The benefit of this is that it connects the individual and his/her actions to the wider social and economic forces that shape their lives. This approach acknowledges their potential to have an impact on processes of social change. Formal and informal processes in the organization provide the key to revealing their politics. If it were only the specific tasks carried out in community organizations that defined them, their contribution to social change would be minimal. However, the social processes in the organizations are the practices that move in other directions.

There are four traditions within the wider community movement that can act to promote a social change agenda within the new development type organizations—democracy, education, alliance-building, and mobilization. The community sector can draw upon these traditions; they can be resurrected at the same time as organizations carry out other activities linked to services and economic development. Our connection to these traditions helps us sustain a vision of why we organize. This vision is shaped by values of social justice and equality. One of the most important roles of community organizing is to be part of the wider struggle for the redistribution of wealth and power. Organizations can provide the means for citizens to gain a voice.

DEMOCRACY

Democracy is the key element. Community development in all of its incarnations has as a core belief its potential to involve the stakeholders in a democratic process. The rhetoric implies more than the practice, but the opportunity is there to be taken by leaders and staff. They can insist on the active participation of residents, users of service, and staff in the decision-making process in their organizations and in the wider community. Creating a "democratic space" in which those without power can have a voice is a starting point in creating social change. In Browne's (2001) discussion of the social economy and other practices similar to it he argues:

> Although they can be recuperated by neo-liberalism, such experiences present many immediate social benefits in the form of services and social inclusion. They are also one of many potential vehicles for the development of democratic capacities, of the ability to participate fully in society and to be self-governing— a process of cognitive and ethical transformation.

They offer glimpses of a more democratic way of governance. (p. 98)

Without this dimension, community organizations become professional services, and those faced with difficult personal and social situations become passive clients. If democracy is the starting point, it cannot be the only goal. It provides the means of creating a culture of opposition, based on active citizens. Up to this point, my argument is similar to the writers I cited above. The difference is that the processes that support democracy have to be extended outward toward external issues and structures. In other words, local democracy is the starting point for recapturing the other three traditions of community organizing.

EDUCATION

Education, which happens in a variety of ways in community organizations, contributes to social change processes. It is important to understand these organizations as sites of both potential and actual learning. Community organizers can gain understanding of process from the work of adult educators. Regardless of the formal mandates and goals of their organizations, they provide opportunities in which participants at all levels can learn to use experience to contest their social situations and engage in a variety of new activities in order to build social solidarity and to act in a collective way to promote social change. Foley (1999) describes the type of learning in social movements as:

> informal and often incidental—it is tacit, embedded in action and is often not recognized as learning. The learning is therefore often potential, or only half realised.... we need to expose it. In doing this it helps if we understand that people's everyday experience reproduces ways of thinking and acting which support the often oppressive status quo, but the same experience also produces recognitions which enable people to critique and challenge the existing order. (p. 4)

He goes on to argue that "the learning of oppositional, liberatory [ideologies] are central to the processes of adult education" (p. 4). Building on the everyday experiences of those participating in community organizations, a variety of educational opportunities are possible. Cervero and Wilson (2001) discuss three aspects of political adult education that can be translated into the struggle for knowledge and power. The first they describe as "the political is personal"—a learner-centred view. It focusses on individual change through a consensus-based strategy. This parallels a service approach, and, although drawing on the voices of those involved, it is limited to that. The second, defined as "the political is practical," is similar to the pragmatic practice of community organizing. The goal here is to help people learn how to get things done, how to mobilize resources within the existing limits of power. In the context of community organizations, the lessons learned are about making limited changes and working for the interest of the organization or program. These are useful in preparing people to engage in the world of day-to-day politics and, at the same time, can promote a belief that politics is defined within those pre-existing limits. In contrast, the authors define the third viewpoint as "the political as structural," using adult education as a way to support the redistribution of power. This is the crucial dimension. In all aspects of work in the community, opportunities arise that lend themselves to provoking political discussion and unmasking power relations. Even if the primary function of the organization is not that of mobilization, people come for a variety of reasons related to wider social and political processes. Activities such as talks and workshops on current issues with invited guests provide an example of these activities. Foley (1999) notes that learning opportunities are contradictory, providing both limits and possibilities. In the new community development practices, there is a lot of pressure for social integration as opposed to social change, but the possibilities are there.

We can see from the example of Chic Resto-Pop, discussed in Chapter 2 (see pp. 52–55; and also Church, Fontan, Ng, and Shragge, 2000) the tension within an organization developed for conventional goals and whose aims can be understood as social integration rather than social change. However, at the same time it was prepared to challenge the government over its training program regulations and to mobilize the wider community to do so. In addition, representatives from Resto-Pop participated in several "community tables" that acted as a voice for wider concerns and pressure on the government over their demands. The wider culture of the organization became linked to the community movement and thus promoted social solidarity and collective action.

Educational practice can take many forms; it begins with an understanding that the problems and issues confronted locally have their origins in patterns of inequality and injustice, for which solutions cannot be found locally. Community organizations can play a role in promoting wider changes. For instance, in Montreal in 1999, a coalition of groups and individuals set up a mock trial to judge the federal government guilty for caving in to the interests of the banks and corporate interests and ignoring job creation and income for the poor in its 1999 budget. It was attended by approximately 200 individuals, members of the groups that organized the event. There are many creative ways to reach people that counter the conservative bias in the mainstream media that attempts to convince us that there are no choices.

BUILDING ALLIANCES

Even if the primary mandate of an organization is service provision or development, it does not mean that there is no space to participate in other activities. The most effective way to do this is through participation in alliances with other organizations at the local level. By breaking down isolation, organizations can step outside their usual boundaries and take on new issues and activities. Alliances contribute to the creation of a base of social power and have the potential of allowing individual organizations to go beyond their specific interests and problems to raise common concerns. An example of this process is the coalition of organizations in a working-class neighbourhood in Montreal that has drafted an alternative urban development plan to put forward local priorities and challenge those of the city administration.

Organizations can join together to promote both local and global causes. At the local level, these groups can speak for the neighbourhood or sector as the most representative body with a legitimate local voice. The organizations—service and voluntary—can move beyond their specific agenda and involve themselves in the process of building power, even if that is not their formal mandate. However, there is a danger. These alliances can become "organizations of organizations," even if they have no base of active members or are unable to mobilize their constituency. Alliances, therefore, can become the representatives of community organizations rather than the catalyst for the mobilization of residents. Organizations, through their staff or a few volunteers, substitute themselves for active citizens. Indirectly, this weakens the process. If the primary goal of the process is to build power through numbers of people, then representation by organization undermines this goal. Further, organizations have a vested interest in survival which can compromise the more explicit political agendas of others in the wider community.

MOBILIZATION

If there is one important lesson on the potential of community organizing, it is the principle that large numbers of people working together with specific demands can have a voice in the process of social change. It is the power of people that matters. Whether it is the recent struggles against globalization or the marches against war in Iraq, such as those in Montreal that attracted 150,000 and 250,000 people in February and March 2003 respectively, or other forms of opposition such as the sit-ins used to gain civil rights or to better social or economic conditions, the power is in the numbers. That is the long and short of it. Trade unions can withhold their labour to try to negotiate better conditions, but community organizations have only one real source of power and leverage—large numbers of people acting together. This might sound overly simplistic, but I believe it is fundamental and has to be stated clearly so that, when one gets to the complexities, the principle stands out. Other forms of practice and action create a critical consciousness and confidence in people.

Neither action organizing nor community development are inherently the better approaches to encouraging democracy or learning. It is the way they link to other movements and struggles that matter. It is their contribution to democratic opportunities and a critical social analysis that makes a difference.

APPENDIX: CONFLICTS AND COMPLEXITIES OF CED, A DIALOGUE

I addressed some of the complexities and conflicts that CED practitioners face in the following extract from a dialogue I had with staff and board members of 761 Community Development Corporation (CDC), a community economic development organization in Toronto. The content presented below is shaped by issues and questions raised by the people there.

Question: Are there ways that corporate culture can be adapted to our purposes, or, by applying this approach, do we risk losing our own vision? So it's not just the "why," it's the "how to do" a social economic development thing, recognizing that the dominant understanding is corporate.

ES: The first issue raised was how do we do business through CED in a way that's different from and not just reproducing the models that we know are out there in traditional business development. The context is the beginning point. We live in a society in which there is rapidly growing social inequality, in which it is increasingly difficult for people at the bottom to survive, at least partly because working-class, blue collar, unionized jobs have disappeared. Through those jobs, people were able to support themselves and often their families. This is less and less the case, and people are being driven to the margins financially. On top of that, we live in a society where we have rapid globalization, so we have a push of industry outwards, using the world as its source of labour. At the same time, the remaining jobs in our society are polarized between high-paying work with more and more people stuck in cheap labour. Along with these changes, we have a very powerful message from those in power: the way people are going to survive is through the creation of their own initiatives. We have a peculiar kind of tension in our society between a coercive monitored workfare and "survive by creating your own kind of business" ideology. We're either going to regulate poor people or we're going to turn them into little capitalists.

So how does CED fit into all of this? Through CED we try to find ways to create enterprise. Do we buy in to this new entrepreneurial push by government and by business? Do we really buy into the mythology that, somehow, if people were smart enough, and worked hard enough, and had adequate technical and financial support, they could create their own little thing and get themselves out of poverty? At the same time, we know that there is a very high rate of failure of small businesses in our society, that there are relatively few jobs created in this process, and that those that are created tend to be low-paying and unstable.

Along comes the community movement with its legacy of struggles for social justice and its critique of the market as an effective means of solving social problems. Most in this movement assume that the government has a fundamental obligation to provide basic health care, housing, and income. Traditionally, the role of the community was to pressure the state to try to make sure that happens. We have that tradition on the one hand, and then we're drawn towards this entrepreneurial thing on the other. So we're stuck in a hard place. I think it comes back to these questions: what does CED mean? Can we really do something that's different through business development? Do we have to reproduce the corporate model to do economic development? At the same time as asking these questions, I have a basic premise for this discussion; that is, CED will neither have the capacity to alleviate poverty except perhaps for a few individuals, nor will it replace the loss of industrial jobs that have disappeared. Our basic question then is: what can CED contribute to the struggle for economic and social justice and how can this happen? I don't have definite answers. I have participated on several CED organization boards and in many related activities. I was involved at the beginning of the Montreal Community Loan Fund and saw it grow from a dream into a reality, the same with loan circles for low-income women. I was also a member of the board of directors of the CED corporation in my district and saw it shaped more by government policy and directives than by local needs and visions. My reservations about being on the community CED board, and one of the reasons that I left, was because a tremendous amount of energy was being put into individual and small group training for the labour market and traditional small business development. Some of the small businesses were succeeding quite well, with four or five jobs being created. I am not against that, but that isn't what I thought CED should be about. Even with those success stories, we still have to face the questions of "what are we doing differently?" and "are we just going to reproduce a small business development model?"

One of the achievements of small business development is that it can reach groups that do not have access to either credit or the technical or other resources necessary for small business development. For example, the CED corporation with which I was involved serves an ethnically and culturally very diverse population, with many new immigrants that don't have access to capital and technical resources. Thus, the organization does play an important role by bringing resources and support to groups that otherwise would be much weaker in the local economic community. But what's changing? In the current context, the central issues in our society—the lack of work and the absence of a collective voice against highly concentrated economic and social power—will not change through this process. Our approach, to use social work terms, is casework;

that is, working to fix up individual lives without challenging the causes of the problems themselves.

Question: I would like a multi-level approach so that, for example, people within particular communities, especially communities that have been traditionally very marginalized, do start to have a sense that business development is not some mythical thing that only particular people can do. That we all can master certain skills and learn how to control, or better control, our fate. So, in that sense, I think that CED is a very good tool, and looking at keeping resources within a community or getting greater control over your resources is a great goal, especially because the tendency right now is globalization. But I would like to see a two-tiered or multi-tiered approach, whereby at the same time that a CDC is, for example, helping to stimulate growth from within marginalized communities or partnering up with people in marginalized communities to start up, for example, community businesses—at the same time that's happening, I would like CDC's to look at forming coalitions with other social justice organizations and pressuring and lobbying government bodies or corporations, because that's where the real power is right now, right? I think that at the same time that we're working at a grass-roots level, we also need to have our eye on where the actual power is in our society, look at lobbying and pressuring for real change, and be very open about the politics of the organization and clearly state: "This is our class analysis, this is our race analysis, this is our CED analysis," and we need to put that out there clearly.

ES: There are several issues that emerge from these comments. First, I think you're arguing that CED should be part of the social justice movement. There are a tremendous number of tensions around it. It's very hard to live with these tensions while one is engaged in the processes of building community businesses. There are pressures in doing economic development that demand a certain level of commitment of human resources and money, and these activities take on a life of their own. With these obligations it becomes difficult to move toward social justice struggles, especially now that CED has become a "flavour of the month" and is supported by government, at least partly, in my view, because it dovetails with the neo-liberal ideology of solving social problems through the marketplace. Organizations build a stake in protecting their funding and become reluctant to challenge wider social and economic policy. It doesn't mean we shouldn't do it [CED], but we have to learn to live with tension. We have to find ways to participate in wider coalitions and use opportunities to do things like organizing public education meetings with the groups with which we are working and helping members make connections between their situations and wider social and economic issues. I believe that organizing, whether it is for CED or anything else, is about the way people can work together to make sense of their situation and find new alternatives. There is a danger in CED that these alternatives will be defined in very narrow terms of entrepreneurship with its focus on individualized solutions to the much wider issues in our society.

Question: Isn't it about putting control of the access to economic development in the hands of the people who are running it? Like, for example, credit unions, whereby you have the capital resources being controlled by the people who actually run it, and the resources stay within the community. Rather than, shall we say, the small business down the street, which is buying extremely cheap items from China, let's say, so half the resources are going outside the country, and they have minimal numbers of staff, who are making minimum wage, and none of the global craftsmen are making any money. Whereas, if you look at a local business in which the people there are manufacturing a product, they're making money, and the people in the community are buying it, so the resources are staying within the community. Isn't that kind of a paradigm?

Question: The building of commonwealth—if we can circulate one dollar so that all of us benefit from the same dollar, by that exchange we've built that much more of a strong economy. If that dollar takes off outside and we can't capture it, then we've got to find another dollar or produce it from our own resources. The problem is that I don't think that is the stage that CED is at.... I don't think we've got enough, it's not like being a small town somewhere or an Aboriginal reserve where the local economy is whatever you make it. We're so open to the larger beat of the local economy here that can affect our community's economy, that it's hard to see those kinds of benefits. And I think there needs to be other things there.

ES: "Business development is a tool." The question is: a tool for what? There are important lessons that come out of community organizing in general. We hold two sets of interacting goals. One set of goals is what we are trying to achieve; the second is the process through which we work. Both parts share the underlying vision that organizing is a means to redress a basic power imbalance in society and a way to help people who are usually excluded from public participation in decisions that have an impact on their lives to gain a collective voice. Therefore, we have to define both of these goals when we work in CED and in building community business. Following this line of argument, CED practice begins with explicitly defined goals—outcome and process—and an understanding of their interaction. Thus, creating small businesses that work in a market economy and can create a few jobs can be a vehicle that carries the other broader goals. Business development in CED should begin with defining its socially oriented outcomes. These can be shaped by values such as ecology or the meeting of social needs or a redefinition of the workplace for people usually excluded from it. But the processes around that set of goals also have to be explicit. The key question for me is whether or not the process enlarges the opportunities for democratic participation for those involved in the business. At the same time, we need to recognize that in our society there are few democratic practices other than choosing between brands either in the marketplace or in the political sphere. CED needs to be a learning process in which new forms of democratic practice can be tested.

CED has to go beyond simplistic notions of job creation. We should ask: what type of jobs? For CED corporations, I think we have to acknowledge the importance of job creation, but, at the same time, we have to be really careful not to become managers of poverty at the local level. In an era of workfare, the community sector has been "used" to implement policies that keep people poor and without power and moving from one program to another. This is the dilemma: CED has become a strategy of the community sector to do something about poverty. We have to be on our guard against changing the poor through the discipline of monitored, subsidized, dead-end jobs and training programs that lead nowhere except more precarious work and welfare. Governments would be happy and would support CED if it could manage poverty in this way and would help support the creation of a pool of very low-wage workers who could move from one project to another. I think this is the direction of a lot of CED and other parts of the community sector, particularly in Quebec. But we need to highlight social processes in our work. What do people get out of the whole thing? Whose interest is served?

Question: Our relationship to the issues that you're describing is almost completely shaped by how we're all funded. And there's a variety of ways that people around the table here are funded. The way we've been talking about it so far is business on the one hand and these traditions of social justice on the other—but the state is a big player in all of it. I think that's the most tangible struggle that I can feel—really immediate—with the group here in the last few months. It's one thing to try to resolve the tensions between the whole culture in which we live becoming entrepreneurial, and us trying to carry on some kind of social justice tradition, but when you've got the state involvement mixed in with that as well, life becomes really dicey in terms of even telling who the good guys are from the bad guys.

ES: There's an interesting pamphlet called "In and Against the State" (1979). It argues that our jobs, or the funding we receive, constitute one of our primary relationships with the state. Thus, we are simultaneously in and part of the state, while, at the same time, we find ourselves opposed to the forms of political and social relationships that are imposed by the state. It's a relationship of struggle, rather than being "good guys and bad guys." We have to assume that there is always tension, an oppositional tension, with the state. It doesn't mean that you don't win or you don't engage, but it means that you don't assume that the state is on our side in a fundamental way. It's about power, it's about how we organize ourselves, and it's ongoing. It is a mistake to assume that the state is politically neutral; the state is shaped by the interests of the dominant powers in the society and is concerned with establishing and maintaining the conditions of those ruling relationships. It is within these relationships that social and political struggles are played out.

Question: I think that part of the difficulty is that it [the state] also separates us from one another, so that getting a sense of collectivity in these conditions is really difficult. And that if it was clearly "us" against "them," hey, I can struggle with that, I can live with the tension. But it's more splintered than that.

Question: When you talk about living with tension among these various forces, I think sometimes we also get an individualized sense of what that means, like we have to somehow personalize it or tough it out in terms of what we go through here. I need to get a stronger sense of how other kinds of organizations as organizations rather than as individuals might help us collectively with those tensions.... I think that one of the things that happens here is that we don't know how long anyone is going to be here, we don't want attachments to one another.

ES: The divide and rule strategies of the state are particularly powerful. People are always competing for scarce resources controlled by different levels of government. The state has fragmented people, partly through social programs and categories—there's always a creation of new categories by programming. You could probably each tell me what budget line you're on, which corresponds with a program line and then a policy, which someone in Queen's Park or Ottawa has decided. So it goes from policy down to a program, through someone's budget, gets even more fragmented in your organization, and then you've got to negotiate your little piece with them. And everyone around the table is sitting with a different little piece. And it creates enormous tensions.

This is all part of the new welfare state, a combination of cutbacks and drawing in of the community sector to provide services and manage social problems. The government is developing what I would call a flexible welfare state. That is, the government no longer wants to administer social programs through large, unionized, stable bureaucracies. That model allowed people to have job security, a union to protect them, and a livable salary. So, in the current context, the people who work in this new area called CED also work in this new universe where everything is short term. Workers are expected to help create community businesses, generate new forms of social empowerment, and survive on contracts and grants. How do you live so precariously? What kind of commitments do you have to support each other through that? How do you manage budgets? The starting point is the collective management of your own affairs so that the "just in time" policies of the state do not act to divide and rule the people who work in your organization. We cannot talk about democratic and empowering processes in CED unless these also exist in the organization that is promoting these activities.

This is one of the big differences between many of the CED organizations in Quebec and what I have seen here [in Ontario]. In Quebec, the community economic development corporations have been recognized, structured, and funded by the state. They have a formal mandate to administer programs decided upon and defined by the provincial government and administered through these organizations. They can be seen as "para-governmental." As a consequence, their employees, unionized in some cases, tend to have more stable working conditions and, despite some instability, can plan their activities for a period that is longer than the life of a short-term grant. Some of these organizations remain aloof from the population and are content with the delivery of economic development and training programs. The contrast is striking in Toronto, where there are no large municipal or provincial policies or strategies on CED. This has allowed practitioners greater autonomy but in the context of instability. These tensions are largely constructed from the outside, but there are choices internally in our responses. The government has provided money for CED on a short-term basis and with regular reviews and shifting priorities. As we watch this happen, we need to reassert our values in open discussion in our organizations so that we can make political choices in a way that is explicit. We need to have discussions about the orientation taken by those who fund our work and the impact it will have on the collectivity. Once this occurs, our negotiations and trade-offs will be transparent, and we can decide if the compromises take too much away from our orientation and values.

There are two traditions within the community movement. We've often talked about the protest side, the struggles for social justice. An equally long tradition is creating social alternatives. The community movement has always been at the forefront of creating real options for people that can make a difference in their lives. You can look at the settlement house movement going back to Jane Adams in Chicago. It had both a social justice agenda and a service agenda. It was also concerned with consciousness-raising, social rights, and community-building. The tradition of alternative services comes out of the community movement. You can look at organizations like rape crisis centres and shelters, which have their origins in the women's movement. You can look at community health movements, the creation of alternative clinics of various kinds. I think CED could fit in several ways in that tradition of creating alternatives that challenge the assumptions about service provision. First, the division between providers and receivers is broken, and both have a voice in the running of the organization. Second, the projects that result should encourage radical democratic processes so that participants have real power to shape their work. Third, there is a tendency in service provision to define people as clients rather than social and political actors. Finally, there is a division between service provision and political advocacy and mobilization for social struggles. The challenge is to live in both at the same time.

What are the implications for CED? Organizations, like community economic development corporations, provide the support and resources for the wider community, in this case to create various forms of community businesses. At the same time, we must not lose sight of the primary goal: helping people secure a voice for themselves. Thus, CED is a means of organizing people who are usually excluded from economic decision-making. This is the potential of CED practice. Right now in a rough, experimental kind of way, we're trying to develop new kinds of businesses. I don't know how they're going to succeed. They're not always financially viable without government support, and I think it's a fair claim that they should be government-supported because they are primarily put in place to obtain social objectives. We're setting up something different, and we have to know what's different about it. There are two key elements: vision and democracy.

When I use the word the word vision, it implies that we have to look in several directions at once. We need to look back in order to understand the traditions with which CED can be connected. CED practitioners sometimes get confused and think that they come out of some kind of entrepreneurial orientation—that they're bringing the market to new places. There is a danger if we look in that direction, because we will lose sight of the necessity to use CED as a tool to mobilize and create new forms of not-for-profit initiatives. We must have a vision of the present. An understanding of the political, economic, and social context and how that shapes what is at stake for different groups in the society is central, particularly the way the changes in the economy have had an impact on changing the face of poverty and increasing social inequalities. If we understand the present, and the social forces that shape it, then we can begin to talk about how CED can redress the gaps in wealth and power between the rich and poor and with whom we can work to do this. Finally, we have to look ahead. Where do we want our practice to take us, and how will that contribute to the long-term process of a different vision of society? For me, these questions are the core parts of an exercise that CED organizations should go through in order to shape their practice objectives. If this does not happen, CED will put in place new community businesses, based on a bottom line, that behave in the marketplace in the same ways as do their private-sector competitors. Is it enough to create a few relatively low-paying jobs or uncredentialed training opportunities for those who may not have other choices? If this is the orientation of CED practice, then perhaps our time and resources would be more useful in organizing pressure groups and building broad-based community alliances to challenge current economic and social policy directions.

Democratic practice is perhaps the most important element. Our society provides very few openings for people, especially that large majority with little clout, to take control of their lives. Democratic practice is the way in which people can collectively shape their daily lives. Thus, the way CED practice is conducted is central. Does it give more control to people over their workplace, over the economic and social development of their neighbourhood? Does it connect them with others that share a common political and economic stake in order to build alliances? Business development, thus, is a process of bringing people together to co-manage an aspect of their lives. This is not an easy process, but it is a necessary prerequisite for a social-change oriented practice. Similarly, CED organizations have to bring these struggles to their members, to help them understand how their situation is shared by others and how solutions will not be found through a simple return to an unfettered free market economy with community business as one of the players.

I have my doubts. After working in the field of CED and writing about practice, I see the pressures of the state-supported programs and the dominant ideology of the entrepreneurial culture to be a double whammy for those in CED. I think that many practitioners have little understanding of the origins, traditions, and political role of the community sector. The government has bought into CED, but more from the point of view that it is politically safe and congruent with dominant values and beliefs. CED organizations have learned how to get support but, with a few exceptions, have not been effective at being "political." The challenge is to move in that direction. Vision and democratic practice are the ingredients that will move us there.

CHAPTER FIVE

MOVING FORWARD: NEW VISIONS AND HOPES

The preceding chapters have traced the theory and development of community organizing practice. I have used a mixture of historical and current examples to explore the transition of organizing from opposition to the structures of economic and social power to a collaborative model often tied to service development and delivery. In recent years, with the community development paradigm described in the last chapter, most practice has lost its political edge and become focussed on the internal processes of the organization and the needs of local citizens. In contrast, in the earlier periods, community organizers saw local work as contributing to, and being part of, a wider movement for social change and social justice. I found this transformation to be not a step forward, but to be out of step with its historical roots. I admit to fearing for the future of the community movement as a force for social change.

Events of the past few years—the demonstrations against the forces of globalization and the marches against the war in Iraq—suggest that today's young people *are* engaged in social movements. Beginning in the fall of 1999, I conducted a series of interviews with the new generation of activists, discussing with them continuities and change. Who did I interview? I was not as systematic as traditional research would prescribe, but began talking to a couple of people I knew and moved from contact to contact; in the end, I interviewed individuals who were relatively young—less than 30—or beginning to work professionally as community or union organizers. Most are women, and they come from a variety of economic, ethnic, and economic backgrounds. It was crucial for me that this cohort of new leadership represent a variety of practices; they include those who are involved in mobilizing against globalized capitalism, organizing new immigrants in their workplaces, developing community gardens, organizing on issues of disability, working with young adults, organizing Black parents on school-related questions, building coalitions for older citizens and for health care reform, and working in community economic development. These activities are as diverse as the activists themselves.

Each generation faces new situations and a shifting context. It builds on and modifies previous work, but also moves in new directions as opportunities are created for different forms of practice and opposition. This generation of activists has set a radical agenda and is pursuing it with new forms of action. Confrontations with the promoters of globalized capitalism have escalated, becoming more visible and dramatic. The people I interviewed are profoundly influenced by ideas that shaped my own politics. Although they do not always express their beliefs in the same words as those of my generation, they oppose the structures and relations of power in fundamental and similar ways. At times, they talk about the constraints they feel with their own practice, but their activities and commitments are derived from a desire to struggle for basic changes in the world around them. In the end, I am convinced that the community movement has within it people with a wide vision and analysis who are working for social justice. Their politics and beliefs go beyond many in the older generation who now hold key positions in community organizations.

DESCRIBING AND INTERPRETING PRACTICE

ANTI-CORPORATE GLOBALIZATION

The movement against the power of global capital has captured the imagination of young activists. I began the interviews in the fall of

1999, a few months before the mobilization for "The Battle of Seattle." This was the first major protest against a World Trade Organization (WTO) meeting in North America. Thousands of activists from many backgrounds jammed the streets of Seattle. Street demonstrations and peaceful rallies of both young and old activists were broken up by tear gas and violence from Seattle city police and the National Guard. It was a watershed event that demonstrated that the new youth movement had sophistication in both its tactics and its analysis of the international situation. It was the beginning of a series of similar mass protests that have occurred when leaders from different countries or international organizations meet to promote "freer" trade and neo-liberal policies. One of the interviewees went to Seattle to take part in the demonstrations and describes what the experience meant to her:

> I think Seattle probably pushed me toward being more hands-on and being more directly confrontational with the things I have problems with. Because I think it's really important to educate the vast majority of people who don't pay attention to these things about the basics of why you should care about those powers that be, about becoming more confrontational with the powers that be.
>
> The corporate [world] sells us ideas, like "you need to buy this; you are a passive citizen, you can't participate in a world-changing way, you can't take the leadership, you can't take the initiative, you're just a consumer and we'll sell you what you think you need, and we'll make you think you need it." And I think there's hope because everyone there had been involved in sort of local causes. And then just going there realizing that your local cause fits into this big picture was amazing just to see…. Sort of local to global. And then we come back and get into the local stuff again with a global mindset.

This young activist reflects the growing politicization within her generation. She makes clear links between the local and the global, connections that have shaped struggles on college campuses. The larger enemy is clearly defined as are its manifestations in many aspects of everyday life. This theme was repeated in many ways throughout the interviews.

LABOUR ACTIVISM

Three interview subjects are involved with labour issues. Two are immigrants from the Philippines to Canada and organize among immigrant workers. The other learned about labour organizing in her job in a movie theatre when she participated in the unionization of the employees; her focus since then has been on the working conditions faced by younger workers, particularly lack of access to better jobs held by "baby boomers." She is part of an advocacy group for young workers whose major campaign is against what are described as "orphan clauses" in collective agreements, which protect those already employed and are not extended to new employees. According to her, this type of practice reflects the wider issues facing younger workers such as low pay and irregular, contractual, and precarious employment. She argues that there is an underlying conflict between older workers, who want to protect what they have already gained by collective bargaining, and younger workers, who want jobs. In addition, there are issues of style and culture that separate trade unions and younger workers.

One of the women from the Philippines joined a group that worked with Filipina women. She became involved in a struggle between a company union that represented 2000 workers in a large, successful clothing factory and the Union of Needletrades, Industrial and Textile Employees (UNITE). She was subsequently hired by UNITE as part of a team that organized 15 other companies. She learned some difficult and important lessons in the process.

> Within the unions there is this ... fighting between each other. And it's really bad for the workers, especially at this point when it seems that it's a low point in

the union movement, because it seems that they don't need the union, and then when the unions start fighting between each other, it really gives a bad impression. Because you're supposed to be there for the workers and organizing them, organizing them to fight for their cause.... The struggle has to go beyond the union. And this is what we are trying to do with the workers. I always explain to them that the union is there. But at the same time the union is working within the system, which is limited. And so for them, they have to see that and to think that—yes, we are in the union now; but if we want more, then we have to push for more. They have to see that the union is just part of the labour movement and to think that even in the union the strength is the workers. So they have to really try to organize among themselves. And when they are organized, then the union sees it and the union can go full blast and fight because they know that the workers are behind them. They can push. But if they are not organized, the union has no power.

The other Filipino organizer discussed his entrée into organizing and his vision of solidarity as follows:

I went to work in a factory ... [in Canada] ... when I was a student organizer for a couple of years. And that's when ...you get pissed off every day. You come home from work, you're really tired, and you can't study any more because you're so tired from work. Meanwhile we get paid less. It's real; it's concrete. To the point where I said, "This is where I belong. This is where I want to study and want to organize."

You really do solid political work with this guy [a co-worker] until [he gets] to the point where he sees beyond colour.... And then we do some political work.... Usually the common ground is the work issue, and they start to see beyond the ethnic background. And I just build on issue after issue after issue, and you could see it developing, it's coming out. Then education starts, from the labour code, labour standards to how to organize.... But there was an idea that came up with a fellow organizer and myself to build a centre where it's not only for Filipinos but mostly immigrant workers where you can build community kind of links with each ethnic groups. And it was an Immigrant Workers Center.

Local work through unions is not only the struggle to make concrete gains and improve working conditions, but a way to encourage activism and political education. For all three labour activists interviewed, union organizing is a means to promote a social and political voice for those who are employed at the margins of the labour market.

NEIGHBOURHOOD ORGANIZING

Several of those interviewed are engaged in local work, either in a neighbourhood or on specific concerns. These range from housing rights and tenant organizing, to creating safety through crime reduction, to building community gardens, to preserving the quality of local life by stopping large-scale development projects. However, they do not see their work as limited to the local. A wider vision that connects specific local work to broader social change is a prevalent theme.

One woman draws on some of the older traditions of community organizing to argue that power is the crucial element.

So, I'm interested in power building and, basically, somehow making it so that, first of all, government can't ignore the people who live in these neighbourhoods. And second of all maybe changing the government. So that it's not really asking someone else not to ignore you, but it's having your own say.... And so in the short term, I'd really like to see better political representation and government responsiveness. In the long term, I think there's much bigger issues than that. But in the long term, there's problems with the economic system. And there's a human side of it and an environmental side of it ... at that point it's hard to imagine how to make that jump, [between the local and larger issues] but I feel like, if you keep working ... you know, the next step will come along, and you'll see it when it gets there.... I think I have a sort of basic faith that ... the average person ... can understand how their interest is tied up with someone else's. So you can be self-interested, but I really don't think it's that hard to understand how you can do better if the people around you are doing better.... I think it doesn't take much for people to see that. And I think most of the social gains that we've made are a little bit related to that.

Here is another connection in both theory and practice between local work and the wider struggle for social justice. As was discussed in Chapter 3, local work is not understood as an end in itself but as part of a wider strategy for social change, providing an opportunity for political education. This is illustrated by the following:

I'm watching some of the people who've been involved in the garden for a couple of years becoming politicized over food by being part of the collective garden... who are suddenly starting to think about corporate control and about the structure of the food economy as a result of that.... I see this as a concrete community-building alternative to a corporate-dominated food system and a way of building community around growing food.... I think that the work that I'm doing in the garden in the community development approach is doing that. It's giving people power over their own lives to the extent that they can have it [power] within a larger context where my analysis sees that you have limited power because the bad guys have it.

COMMUNITY ECONOMIC DEVELOPMENT

One of the people I interviewed works in an organization providing credit to businesses with a social vocation. He describes the vision of the organization as follows:

> The stated mission ... is to fight poverty and unemployment, to combat these phenomena. And the tools that it employs to do this are providing capital, access to loans, and technical support and accompaniment necessary for these loans to be successful in developing initiatives that meet our social objectives as well as economic objectives.

However he does not see the businesses as an end in themselves:

> I don't agree with the idea that when you start a business and if it has social objectives, that in and of itself is not sufficient to change the economy. You're doing casework.... I think that you have to push the social agenda further to make it something that is more, to push it to a macro-level. How I see work in that direction is when, for instance, it's two mainly very closely tied phenomena. One would be popular education, awareness, and another is participation. As soon as you have participation, you have increased participation in any kind of system. As soon as individuals start to coalesce around common goals and a common understanding of what it is you have to do to change the situation and make it more suitable for that collective and subsequently for each individual in that collective, then you have the possibility of involving them in positive change.

Once again we see a recurring theme. Practice is not only about the specific outcomes but is a means of reaching people and finding new ways to deepen their social awareness, thus creating new forms of social solidarity.

A VOICE FOR MINORITIES

One woman discusses how, coming out of her own situation, issues of race, oppression, and exclusion have shaped her practice:

> I work mainly with recent immigrants and visible minorities.... We've established a coordination team of mothers. What we do as a team is we go through the entire process of the project; meaning, we look at the development, where we want to take it, what do we have to do to get it there, [we do] outreach, we do training, personal training to help us develop tools [from communication to advocacy] to help us support the parents, other parents like ourselves. We've also just developed some working groups; they're action-working groups to address issues that parents have identified. These issues range from feelings of exclusion *vis à vis* their schools, discrimination, and just an overall overwhelment [sic] of our big educational system and how we can maneuver it, how we can get it to work for us.

COALITION BUILDING

Coalition building on specific issues has a long tradition in community organizing. One activist is working with a coalition of what she describes as "feisty seniors" to contest changes and other issues related to the privatization of health care. Her group uses a variety of tactics such as public demonstrations and occupations of offices, but priority is given to public education and popular education through workshops held in many organizations. In these workshops:

> it's very important for us to go through the one victory that we did have because that is directly the result of public pressure. Then we usually have a session on how people are effected by this themselves, so that we can

> have a discussion to see people's perspectives. It's usu-
> ally very interesting, not only from the point of view of
> getting involved, but also inevitably there are problems
> that come up that we haven't seen before or concerns
> that people have that we didn't see somewhere else....
> And then after that we talk about the general themes
> and the general problems; we talk about access to med-
> ication, for example; we talk about the whole issue of
> pharmaceutical companies and insurance companies
> and how essentially the government is subsidizing
> those companies at the expense of poor people.

Organizing for specific gains is a process of political education. Challenging those with power and winning victories encourages activism and also unmasks how the system operates, how public policies often serve corporate interests. Organizing can be a tool for making gains nonetheless.

SOME COMMENTS

In conducting these interviews, I was impressed by many aspects of the practice that was described to me. These activists have found many ways to engage in the world, many ways to work for social change. Their activities are linked to older traditions, but they reflect a new perspective because of the context they face. Fisher (2001) argues that, as a consequence of globalization and changes in the economy, our lives have become increasingly privatized. He writes:

> ... the world in which community workers live and
> work is increasingly moving away from the public, away
> from the social toward a preoccupation with the pri-
> vate. This is the new and challenging context for con-
> temporary community organization: How to practice
> social work in a world increasingly antagonistic to the
> public. How to create empowered public citizens in a

context that increasingly values independent and private consumers, workers and family members. (p. 103)

The emphasis on competition and the drive for individualized solutions to economic and social problems, combined with irregular and insecure work situations, make organizing more difficult today. In addition, as discussed in Chapter 4, many community organizations have turned away from organizing and mobilization and have looked to services as a way to solve social problems. The people interviewed challenge both the dominant viewpoint in the society and in the community sector, bringing a political consciousness with an analysis of interest and power into practice, along with a vision about the necessity of linking local organizing to basic social change. They have a commitment to grassroots work. They are neither representing people nor providing services for them. They are actively recruiting and creating situations in which people can act collectively to pursue common interests. The political perspectives that shape their practice are more influenced by the search for a comprehensive social agenda.

One aspect that I find particularly important is the emphasis on political education. Particular projects and activities have provided the means and the forum for raising ideas and debates about wider social and economic issues. Many see the centrality of the corporate economic power and find ways at the local level to challenge it, either through action or education. Political work links the local with the global and forms a common agenda across projects, organizations, and activities.

BECOMING AN ACTIVIST

The next question I asked the interviewees was how they became organizers and activists. Based on interviews with community organizers, Mondros and Wilson (1994) found a combination of intentional factors and happenstance that contributed to the decision to enter the field. These include:

1. Family background. Families provide a world-view, a set of values and beliefs about people and society, and teach about social conditions that legitimate activism. This continues to influence beliefs and supports practice.

2. Personal experience. Activism or volunteering in high school or earlier, such as working on political campaigns or in service clubs, shape attitudes in youth.

3. Education. In college, exposure to course materials generates greater social and political consciousness, while at the same time it provides opportunities for activism.

4. Frustrating or negative experiences. Experiencing these in one setting coupled with development of awareness in another leads to the consciousness of common goals and the need to move into organizing to develop a common goal or analysis.

5. Oppression. Personal experience of oppression or deprivation can be a powerful motive to organize.

6. Becoming a paid worker in a social organization. A transition from a powerless victim to a self-confident salaried activist in the same organization supports a choice to work as an organizer.

These themes provide a useful way to organize the material that emerged from the interviews.

FAMILY BACKGROUND

Most of those I interviewed credit the support of their family whose social values were, at least, not hostile to organizing and social activism.

> I think that there is tacit encouragement. My family is not a family of activists, but now, when I look back at what my parents have always said, I think that they're

very liberal in most social issues.... They're very critical [of politics], especially now of [Ontario's Con-
servative] Harris government and everything that
they're doing. So that's always come out and has
shaped my values a lot.... They've been supportive of
my activities, I think. And allowed me to pursue different directions. So [they were] accepting but they
weren't leading me toward activism in any way.

One woman discusses the impact of her mother's commitment
and the way that it encouraged her to become involved in the struggle for social justice.

It was just the way I was raised. My mother is a phe-
nomenal woman in her own way.... She was at the
Black Community Center in Côte des Neiges.... She
was the administrative assistant. So she had connections to different people who came in ... just friends of
my mom, but I remember them giving me an Afro.
My mother used to press my hair and straighten it out
and put it in ponytails. And I remember feeling good
about my Blackness once Rosie Douglas gave me an
Afro.... And I just was surrounded by a lot of strong
men and women who were very confident and very
vocal and expressed not only the greatness that Black
people contributed to Canadian society but also the
challenges, the obstacles and racism, and what it
means and how it manifests. My mom ... struggled to
put food on the table, you know, the lack of opportunity and just letting us know that it's not because you
can't do it, it's because you don't have the chance to do
it. So I think that's the roots that nurtured me.

Another traces her radicalism back to her parents who she describes
as "very critical academic Catholics ... very social justice oriented."

So I grew up with a lot of social justice values that I learned in a Christian context that I translated into a secular world. That's where I understand where my bite for social justice comes. Whenever I go to a demo, associative memory, I start singing the peace songs of the Nuke rallies that I was brought to when I was a kid. And then I had a couple of formative experiences. When I was a teenager, I went to a summer camp that was run out of a College in Boston ... that had a lot of discussions about capitalism and patriarchy and that kind of stuff. So I got all my appropriate political brainwashing at a young age. But I think I had a strong predisposition toward all of that. But then I got a lot of ideology when I was 14, 15, 16, and I sort of took that on my shoulders and was mad at injustice, and patriarchy was bad.

EXPERIENCES IN HIGH SCHOOL AND YOUTH GROUPS

These early experiences help create critical consciousness and support decisions to work for social justice, but they are not the only factor. Experiences during adolescence either in high school or in youth groups opened people to issues of injustice.

I think, for me my political ideas are very much tied into the Reagan years and the nuclear arms race that was going on.... It started out very innocently, but when I was 11, I met these kids from Hungary, and ... we had this kind of basic understanding that on TV it seemed like you weren't really supposed to like people from the eastern-bloc countries and ... they were from behind the Iron Curtain and ... we ended up talking about what did people there think, and what do people here think, and we came to this conclusion that it was pretty stupid, the whole Cold War, at a basic level.... But it started from there. I kind of got involved in the anti-nuclear movement in Ottawa. I was about 13. And it was really a big thing, when the Peace Camp was on Parliament Hill.... There was lots of civil disobedience, but being 13, I didn't get involved in that. There was a big network, and I was involved in a student network. It was all student-run. And so we got to meet teenagers from all over the city who were interested in the same stuff. It evolved into other things. And ... discrimination and racism, was always something that I was concerned about and was involved with, from when I was young.

EXPERIENCES IN UNIVERSITY AND TRAVEL

For this person and others interviewed, activist experiences in high school stimulated them to look for ways to engage when they entered college or university. During their years in higher education, these activists and community organizers either became politicized or enhanced their previous involvement. One found university to be a way to overcome what he described as a "bourgeois family."

My parents had a big house and my dad had a big job. My mom, for most of my childhood, was at home, did volunteer work.... [I had] what I consider to be a very banal childhood and adolescence.... And then I go to college ... I think half the student population had its own car. I started working on the student paper. I started being exposed to a lot of different ideas at the time, which you don't get in high school. And I think that's perhaps where I started thinking about issues, more from the student's point of view of student rights, and always it's the students against the administration. We were very strong about that, making sure that our services were provided properly and in a way that reflects our fees that we pay for them. And always that

sort of confrontation with the establishment, being in
the student paper and playing a role there because
you're always sort of using that soap box to make a
number of very sometimes empty but very loud claims
about student life.

For another, the university provided events that had a politicizing
impact. She tells this story:

[The] Principal [of the] University had an impact on
why I became an activist. Actually now that I'm thinking about it, really a big impact, because I was a true
believer in lobbying, like a real true believer in the success of like rational argument and discussion.... What
I'm thinking is so logical to me, if I just talk to the principal he'll understand. You know, I really had that
belief. I organized that Future Visions conference ...
and invited him ... as well as inviting students to write
papers on their opinions of the future of the university.
So we had this like, you know, students and, students
and administrators shar[ing] vision. And I thought, oh,
this is good, this is the way that I like to do stuff. And I
realized that with all my effort, that he never swayed ...
you know, not like respectful of alternate opinions and
so set in his ways and so conservative. And I kept on
hitting a brick wall constantly with this guy. And that's
what radicalized me. Because I realized that lobbying
was not going to work, no matter what we did, no
matter how much we tried, he didn't care really, and
just made semblance of listening, but didn't actually
listen at all. And so that's one of the reasons I radicalized and I stopped organizing that kind of thing [civil
disobedience], with that kind of goal.

These experiences are formative. They act to shift understandings of the world, and, more importantly, they provide an opportu-

nity to learn collective work and to find social solidarity. They create the ideological perspectives and the skills that can be taken into later activities, organizations, and struggles.

Travel, particularly through programs of work in developing countries or in poor communities in Canada, contributed to the politicization of several of those interviewed.

> I went to Yellowknife on an exchange trip, and it was for me a really interesting experience.... We talked a lot about poverty on that trip. And there was like a class that went with it. We talked a lot about oppression and the history of relations between Aboriginal communities and other communities and all that's one example, a huge example, of oppression in Canada. And I think going there just made that more tangible for me.

Following university this same woman lived in Japan for a year, traveled to Asia, and worked in a Tibetan refugee camp. During her trip she began to reflect on her experiences:

> I think living in Japan was an important experience for me because I lived in a very small town. I was the only non-Japanese person.... It was a very difficult place to live as a blond woman. It was an excellent experience for me, even though it was difficult sometimes because it was my first experience of being treated in a particular way, even though it was artificial in the sense that I was there for only a year and there was a lot of privilege. I considered myself a feminist when I went there, but it made me think a lot about my views on everything. It made me think a lot about what I thought about how societies are organized, what I valued.

University and travel are the opportunity for young people to examine the world and figure out their place in it. For those I interviewed these experiences were the impetus for later activism. This relationship is not necessarily directly connected. There are thousands who go to university and travel who do not become activists and/or community organizers. However, the group that I interviewed was open to the experience and were able to reflect upon it and see the world as a place of both injustice and opportunities to do something about it. The two go together.

PERSONAL EXPERIENCE OF OPPRESSION

A few of the people I interviewed point to personal experiences of oppression or negative experiences as a trigger for the activism that shapes their lives. For example, one became active as a result of her own disability and the lack of access to university offices.

> When I hit university and experienced some quite glaring discrimination along with other students with disabilities, we decided to take action. And the event around which I really started to be an activist was the complaining and protesting against the fact that the Office for Students with Disabilities was not accessible. Sort of an irony of all ironies, it was up a flight of stairs. And so we managed to shame the university into moving it within a few months. But that is where I really started learning about getting people together and organizing and communicating and getting more people on side.... And so I felt that I'm right, and this situation is wrong, and I just can't let this continue. I have to stand up and say, no, you can't get away with this. That's why I was able to be so passionate about it because I truly believed in the cause and the injustice was so glaring that I couldn't let it just slide.

Racism for another activist worsened an already sad family event and provoked action.

My brother was killed at ... school during recess time. He was run over by a snow blower.... They gave her [the mother] $2,000, which is I guess what the value of his life was worth. He was a nine-year-old Black boy. And back then Côte de Neiges was the ghetto. And I remember a lot of other mothers and kids marching up and down the street and saying it wasn't acceptable. So I just remember her [mother] always speaking up for injustices and always saying "I know my place; it's right beside any other human being." Now it's embedded in my soul, who I am, what I can do and what I don't have to put up with.

A woman who became a trade union organizer and works with immigrants lived through the immigrant experience herself. She found strength in her people and in their history.

I was growing up during the time when the movement for social change was really starting, and it's being started by the young people.... I think I was in grade six at the time. So I was really young to join in, but there was lots and lots of demonstrations. At the time they saw that the enemy was Marcos. But there's a lot of the anti-imperialist things that were happening. So after that there was Martial Law. I was graduating from high school at that time. And I really just feel that the people who were involved in it have so much courage and so much commitment to fight for social change. And see that it's so, the army was very powerful, and the US dominance was really present in the Philippines at that time. So I said these people, how can they do it? And then Marcos was out, and people thought that the change would come, and several government changes later the problem is getting bigger and bigger; and people are going out of the country more and more.

Then I came to Montreal. And in Montreal I was lucky enough to, well work is work [as a domestic], but with my boss I was there for six years. They sent me through school, like whenever I could manage. So right away, I went to a driving school because also they need me for the kids, to drive the kids around, to bring them to school in the morning.... in December I had my license.... So I picked up all these women that's on the road to go back to Côte des Neiges, because most Filipinos live in Côte des Neiges. So that's how I got involved again.

THE ACTIVIST BECOMES AN ORGANIZER

Working as a community/union organizer requires strong social commitment and a capacity to work well with others and to sustain one's confidence. For many this is too difficult. However, the best educator is experience and action. One woman describes how she was able to develop the strength to act effectively:

[I had the idea to start] a youth centre, which addresses the needs of youth from age 13 to 17. So I started working on that.... I had no idea of "politics" is what they call it.... But I mean we met with the police chief, myself and a white man. And I would talk, and the man wouldn't look at me, and he wouldn't respond to me. And so my colleague would talk, and he would look at him and respond to him. Finally, I just looked at him [colleague] and said, "Forget it, you don't say another word. Either this man speaks to me or we don't speak." And that was the first, challenging the structure.... I'm just saying, "That's it. If he can't speak with me, how is he going to have the interest of our children at heart, if he even does. We're going to have to force the issue." It worked out pretty well.... And he actually started to give me eye contact and give me the respect that I believed I deserved. And we actually had a pretty good relationship after that; he helped us with fundraising and so forth. But I think I helped break some of his stereotypical views because I wasn't going to be a "yes massuh," that's not where I'm coming from. And once he realized that I wasn't going to just pretend that those dynamics weren't going on, he had to change his strategy, which means he had to look at and address me and speak with me and give me the respect that I deserved.

We learn lessons about power and the way to get it by challenging those with authority and winning. This in turn builds leadership and pushes activists to go further. It is an essential lesson. It is a belief that people can take control over their lives, articulate demands, and challenge those who, because of rank and position, seem to be untouchable. Learning to be an organizer starts out with taking a leadership role and then teaching others that they, too, are able to lead.

Gender inequality is still an issue for women determined to play leadership roles, particularly in the presence of male organizers. For the women I interviewed the struggle around gender is important. However, none of them work for projects or organizations that deal exclusively with women. The incident described below brings home the difficulties faced by women in organizing activities in terms both of personal safety and their relationships with male organizers.

One time I really felt unsafe. I had a partner, but we went into this building … that was like a rooming house, but it was not housing-code standard. Hallways were all winding, and it was pretty dark, and there would be doors where you weren't expecting them; it was like a maze. And it was scary, and it was all men who lived there pretty much, I didn't see any women when we were there…. We did our door-knocking, telling about a community meeting. [Afterwards] we were meeting everyone back at the donut shop to talk. I said something like, "You know, that was the first time that I have really felt uncomfortable, I was kind of scared in there … [but] we met a couple of people who I thought were going to come out. I think it went all right, people talked to me." And one of the senior organizers [male] said, "Well, you know [why] all the guys came out to talk to you, you know why people are going to come to your meeting … because every guy in that building is going to be dreaming about fucking you."

I was so shocked that he said it that I, couldn't respond.… It just kind of made clear to me that he didn't really think that I should be doing this at all. And he said it in front of all the young people, so it was also kind of humiliating to me in front of everyone.

And then I was kind of mad at him … he was basically telling us what the next steps were, he wasn't asking us what we thought, he was just telling us. So I started to kind of argue with him. But I wasn't arguing, I was asking questions. Well what about this, what about that? And he just said, "It's none of your business, you don't know what you're talking about." And then I was shocked.

Although this experience was rather obviously crude, the same woman found more subtle sexism in other work situations.

I had another work partner there who was more like the tame sexist, the not-so-bad sexist type of guy.… He's not out to get you exactly, but he's more like the gentleman sexist, you know what I mean, he always wanted to open the door for me, and he always wanted to lift heavy things, and so it wasn't like a major problem, it was just come on, get over it.… And the way he would talk about the members as well, like … treat them like ladies …it was just his perspective was that men are this way, women are that way.… The partner that I was talking about, he thought I was his secretary. He was my partner, he had the same job, I'd been there longer than him, and he would ask me to type his papers for him.... And one time I said to him, "Why do you think that I'm going to do your typing?"... And he said to me, "I have more important things to do." And I said, "What do you mean?" [He says] "I need to be out meeting the people. You're good at typing, and you're good at writing, so you do that work. "

Those in community organizations need to understand that the feminist struggle is far from over and that women still experience both overt and subtle oppression from their male colleagues. The culture of community organizing must be transformed to allow greater opportunities not only for women but for new immigrants, the disabled, and other minorities to take positions of leadership.

One of the challenges facing those working in the community is to sustain their activities over time. One young organizer summarizes the challenges and the ongoing commitment.

This is the kind of work that I want to do. I want to be working at a job that I feel is useful. Useful for me has to go beyond a social work job, useful for me means contributing in some way to social change.... When I first started, you read about group work or the process of social change with the group or democracy and practice or all those things. And it's a million times harder in practice that it ever seems to be on the page. But that's an invaluable lesson and those are things that apply elsewhere in my life anyway, even outside of work. It's much larger than work for me. It's not just work for me. It's everything that I do.

This is easier to do if one does not have any personal obligations beyond the self. In addition, in many settings, there are pressures to work long hours, attend countless meetings (often in the evening), and be involved in a variety of voluntary activities. The difficulty comes when one changes one's personal life. Is it possible to rebalance activities to take into account those changes?

> My own core values presently are in major overhaul ever since I got married last year ... because I discovered what family is about, what raising children is about as well.... It didn't blow away a lot of my values; but it, in a very short period of time, required me to develop a whole new set of values that I didn't necessarily have to think about.... Before everything else you have to provide, you have to be in a position to provide and also be open to receiving from those who are your immediate family, your children and your spouse. My personal values now are telling me that the energy that I have must be first and foremost to maintain that family unit in a harmonious and healthy environment. And anything I do now is to do that. So whereas before ... it was only myself and my own values as someone who was committed to social and economic justice ... if at some point in my life, it could be in a month, it could be in a year, I find that my doing this kind of work is impinging on my family's health and well-being, I'm going to have to start thinking about doing something else, and looking for work that corresponds to my values, the values that were there before, but at the same time still respect the new values that I've adopted for myself which is that I love the people in my family and want whatever's best for them.

Involvement over the long-term requires balance. It is not always easy to achieve both personal and political satisfaction. The "revolution" is not a simple act or event and is unlikely to be around the corner. If activists and organizers are to grow gray in their work, the balance between the personal and political is one of their primary challenges.

SUSTAINING WORK

I asked all of those I interviewed how they sustain their work. This raised many issues, especially dealing with the anger generated by. discovering injustice both at a personal and wider social level. One woman describes this feeling and how she has learned to respond to it, maintain her activities, and keep herself centered.

> When I was younger, I got all of these ideologies in my head, and I was an angry kid. I listened to loud music, and I was outraged toward the social injustice in the world; I was outraged; how could I not be outraged? And I don't really think that that helped me. I don't really thing that that made me a happier person. I don't think it improved the quality of my life. I thought Marxism was great, and I thought that we had to create economic equality; it was about economics. People needed to have the same economic power. But that's empty. What are you going to do with economic power; if you're going to have a space to live your life, you have to create something; you have to be a person. Being a person is a much more complex and rich and wonderful thing than just having enough money to buy groceries, although that lets you do a lot of things. And so in my personal experience, I was radicalized early and I think that was maybe emotionally self-destructive in some ways…. What was missing? Value in myself and other human beings and looking at human experience and relations between people and art and culture….

Building a supportive network through family, neighbourhood, and mentors helps to keep one going in one's work. One organizer described this as follows:

> People who are a lot like me—neighbours, friends, all in that same community. A lot of them are friends for

at least the last ten years. And so we've been going through this process of discovering ourselves and the need that we have to change what's wrong in our society so that our children could benefit at least. And I often talk to somebody who's very near and dear to me, and she helps me out a lot ... she helps me when I begin to doubt what I'm doing and always encourages me. And then there's of course my children, and my mom. She never criticizes me; she's always there ... if I need to sleep in, something as little as that. Because often when you give so much of yourself to help others, there's no replenishing oneself. So she lets me get back on track. "Never mind a meeting, go to a movie...." And my children are just so great. And I look at them and I see their potential and I want to do whatever I can to make sure that they're able to get the opportunities that they deserve.

Shared beliefs are also a key element in keeping up the energy necessary to do this kind of work. Acknowledging that what organizers do is not regular work helps to validate the work and can contribute to support.

It was hard because I think if you're involved in this stuff, you're going against the grain every single day, and you have to explain all the time, why do you take this approach, why do you believe in this.... And you lose most of the time. So then it's a drag to come home at night and have to defend yourself one more time. You kind of want someone who just understands and you don't have to ... argue with them and try and convince them that you're doing the right thing.... if you want to do it, if you want to keep doing this as a ... career, there's going to be a lot of things that come up in your life that will require some give and take from the other person, which I think come up no matter what you do, but if they don't agree with why you're doing it, it's going to make it hard for people to go back and forth on it. If they don't really think that community organizing is a useful way to make social change, then they're not really going to want to trade off looking after a kid at night.

Another approach is to keep personal and political lives joined, with no separation between the two. This organizer has succeeded in building a political community, one of activists, family, and friends. This is not an easy task in a society as fragmented as ours. His commitment is total.

This soldier told him [a friend] that "communism is not a shirt where you can take it off any time you want or if you don't feel like wearing it any more." From the beginning, I was integrating my organizing and my political work with my life already even before I was married. And practically I organized my wife, my girl-friend at that time, so I organized her to be part of the student group until she became active. And now she's a person of the Filipino women's organization. And she also regards organizing the Filipino women, domestic workers here, as part of her day-to-day life. You go home, you get calls from people about this, about that, and asking you stuff. So it's not, actually no, it's not separate.... You don't look for political support, you build it. You build it through your organizing until you build up a lot of political friends that you talk to.

At times, there are periods of despair and then new activities revitalize activism.

I guess maybe I do have a community. A lot of my friends are activists. Yeah, it's true that frequently we'll find ourselves talking about our personal battles and hearing about what they're up to is certainly reassuring and strengthening.... Knowing that you're not the only person who believes in certain principles and is willing to go out there and fight and put personal time and energy to further certain goals and to fight against injustice and inequality and so on. Knowing that you're not the only one is very important because I think maybe my low point a year and a half ago was because I'd lost touch with a lot of people who were doing this. And I was feeling very alone in the world, and I just didn't feel very supported. And when you have close people who understand what it is you're doing as an activist too.... I think that you can't do everything alone. And I was definitely going through a period where I was fighting a lot of little battles on my own. And this community neighborhood association that we've created and the battle that we've been fighting has been with such a great group of people that we can only feed off each other. And that's really kept us going and it gave me a lot of strength and energy.

The lesson is universal. Ongoing work in organizing requires support; equally importantly, it requires connections with like-minded people, who share common values. Brian Murphy (1999) describes political work in terms of an "open conspiracy," which has two basic functions: as a reference group and as an action group. The reference group is the key in sustaining activism. He defines it as "a group of individuals who have joined together as a social, emotional, factoral and analytic support network. The group is available for referral of personal/political problems arising from the work of its members" (p. 103). He acknowledges the demands and difficulties facing activists and argues: "The focus within a reference group is on defeating the encroachment of the psychology of inertia by transcending the ambiguity and contradictions, and transforming the dilemmas of inertia through action" (p. 104).

Building our own reference group is a way to sustain organizing and activist activities over the long term. This lesson has been learned early by those I interviewed and each has tried to find his/her own allies and friends that can contribute to their long-term engagement. It is not always easy, but, as one stays involves, the network of allies grows. However, places are needed to meet, to talk, to reflect, and to renew. One such place is the Summer Institute held annually at Concordia University, organized by The Institute for Management and Community Development. During the past ten years, hundreds of community organizers and activists have gathered each summer to learn from and exchange experiences with each other. These kinds of events contribute to a supportive culture for organizing.

RENEWAL OF THE POLITICS OF SOCIAL CHANGE

I began these interviews in a period of renewal. The mobilization against global capitalism had begun. The huge demonstration in Seattle in the fall of 1999, followed by those in Prague and Quebec City, put activism on the map. Articles appeared in the mainstream press not only about the drama of the events themselves but about the lives and political perspectives of the new generation of activists. All of those I interviewed understand their work in the context of international economic power and the dangers it presents for local communities, such as increased poverty and social and economic instability. Many of their practices are in response to changes in work or the welfare state, such as the experience of low-wage, precarious jobs for youth. Similarly, the current experiences of immigration and work in sweatshops are structured by changes in the world's economy. Community entrepreneurship reflects both the lack of jobs and the reduced support by the welfare state for the unemployed and the poor. CED described earlier is an example of an initiative to respond to this changing context. As discussed in Chapter 4, these new business-oriented practices mirror the changing context but do not directly resist it.Perhaps we have turned a corner, at least for a while.

Naomi Klein (2000), in her best selling book *No Logo*, describes the shift as follows:

> Five years earlier, campus politics was all about issues of discrimination and identity-race, gender and sexuality, "the political correctness wars." Now they were broadening out to include corporate power, labor rights, and a fairly developed analysis of the workings of the global economy. It's true that these students do not make up the majority of their demographic group—in fact, this movement is coming, as all such movements do, from a minority, but it is an increasingly powerful minority. Simply put, anticorporatism is the brand of politics capturing the imagination of the next generation of troublemakers and shit-disturbers. (p. xix)

New political practices, put in place by this generation of activists, have been characterized as "people's globalization" or "globalization from below." Starr (2000) writes:

> The basic idea ... is that people all over the world are commonly threatened by environmental degradation, abuse of human rights and unenforcement of labour standards, and that powerful global alliances can be formed to make corporations and governments accountable to people instead of elites.... Instead of wielding the nation-state as a defense against globalization, these movements perceive the need to globalize resistance to match the globalized structure of neoliberal exploitation. (p. 83)

The new movement draws on the traditions of the New Left described in Chapter 3 with its emphasis on face-to-face democracy as a process in organizing, the use of extra-parliamentary opposition, and direct action as a strategy of opposition. In interviews with two of the women, I focussed on their participation in these new movements. I asked about the process of organizing. Here is a description of one campaign, whose initial success prompted further action; the use of affinity groups is characteristic.

It started in '97. It was an organization based on affinity groups ... from different places and [we] closed down Complex G in Quebec City, which is one of the big government buildings where is housed, among others, the Ministry of Education. We were demanding quite a broad platform of demands at the time ... pretty much for the maintenance of multiple social programs for a healthy environment and ... against free trade agreements, etc. It was quite a successful action, we managed to close it down and keep all the workers out that day. And there were no arrests at that action. It was a very interesting action.

From that came the idea of Operation Salami which happened in May '98. It was a blockage of the Sheraton Hotel. At the Sheraton that day there was an economic conference going on, where there were heads of many different countries and corporations talking about globalization and about free trade agreements like the Multilateral Agreement on Investment. At the time, it had been in negotiation for a number of years in secret and had been leaked. And so we closed down the Sheraton Hotel that day, it was sort of, not the same people necessarily, but some of the same people from Plan G. And we managed to keep the number of people out for a number of hours, but then, by about 10 or 11 a.m., the police pretty much cleared the way, arrested 100 people, and the conference continued. But the media coverage was really good and I think it had an impact.

Every person who participated had to be part of an affinity group ... you had affinity with these people, so, you're either friends or you developed affinity

> through exchange…. There was I think about 10 or 15 of us. And we met regularly, to discuss our political positions on things ranging from capitalism to nonviolence to more specific things like what we thought about education…. [We] got to know each other, and then the idea was that one person from that group would be mandated to go to another meeting where there would be one person from every affinity group and that's how decisions would be made…. People would go from the affinity group to the coordinating committee, and then come back always…. And the idea is that no important decision would be made until the affinity group agreed on it.

Face-to-face democratic processes and a federated decision-making process allows small groups to build autonomy and learn to take action together, while negotiating common actions with others.

Another aspect of this new movement has been its effective strategies of education in the context of mobilization and demonstrations. The young woman introduced at the beginning of this chapter describes how and what she learned in Seattle:

> I went early enough to go to the big teach-in; so that was really amazing. I think a lot of people went there to, first of all, learn about the issues and put our heads together with some of the leading thinkers on these kinds of issues from around the world. The panels were really great. The first night was an overview of basic myths about globalization and how it relates to the WTO and what we're here to accomplish. Then they divided up into panels on different topics so that we could learn more in depth about like biotech farms and challenging corporate rule…. And then after each talk there was a smaller discussion session so that people could interact more…. The people on stage didn't want to be above everyone else. They wanted to

really facilitate some sort of dialogue. And a lot of the emphasis was on providing alternatives as in shifting from opposing and exposing to proposing ... charting our own course and not just saying that the course we're on is bad. Because then people will say, "Well, we don't have a choice; this is inevitable." So there was a big focus on alternatives.

Part of my initial motivation was just that the speakers were so good, I wanted to learn more. But basically during the thing [demonstration], the 2,500 people that were there and the speakers were just really keen on getting on to the streets after talking about it. So it was really great. It wasn't just a conference; it was the teaching—[that] was the more appropriate word, because it was like we'll talk and then we'll go on the streets; it was very effective that way. I like it better than just protesting without the thing [teach-in] beforehand too, because then you don't necessarily have the same conviction that you're intellectually in the right. And not everyone would necessarily be on the same page. But they did a good job of laying the groundwork by saying these are the basic things and this is how you can respond.

Education goes beyond understanding the politics of the issues. It is also about preparing for action. Learning forms of actions prepared activists to engage in the events on the streets and, if arrested, in jail. The demonstrations were covered by many television crews so that "the whole world was watching." As a result, these demonstrations against globalization have had an impact on consciousness and have been a source of energy for local work. One person made the following connections:

It's probably no accident that people in my neighbourhood are suddenly finding within themselves the energy and the desire to get together collectively and fight a greater power because we feel so powerless. We feel powerless definitely on the global scale, when you think about the fact that there are probably many multi-national corporations who have the power to control and determine the way the world will work. They have more power than certain countries, certain governments, then you can just despair and feel completely helpless. On the other hand, if you feel that at least in your neighbourhood, in your immediate world you can make a difference, then … I just think there's a parallel, and I think that seeing the protests in Seattle and then Prague and so on, it's that maybe we're seeing this happen more and more. And maybe somehow this is giving people the strength to participate or speak out in their own communities.

The renewal of activism among youth has been a powerful process, bringing together social movements such as the ecology, women's, and some ethnic minorities, as well as older forces of the left including trade unions. This broad-based alliance is fragile but, compared to the organizing of the 1970s, is impressive. As with any social movement, can it be sustained over time? The question of organization and leadership will certainly become difficult, as a movement that manifests itself through large demonstrations cannot sustain these activities for too long. At the same time, the processes of organizing and political education have touched many young people. Local work may be the place where this energy and consciousness is expressed.

Will this new energy, experience and consciousness translate itself into local work and activities or will the movement of young activists play itself out and disappear into the "normalcy" of consumer culture? The radicalism of the anti-globalization movement and its forms of democratic practice conflict with the culture of many community organizations. One organizer expressed her frustration as follows:

I think that a lot of community groups, especially ones that offer services, have become so wound up in the services because of all the cutbacks and because of the pressure on those groups and [so they] have less time for the social action side of it. But it's more important than ever really to me now.... There are really only a handful of groups who do a lot of mobilization work, in some areas more than others.... Some groups, like the seniors groups for example, where there's tremendous power—if the seniors groups were to mobilize strongly for anything that makes a huge impact. Some of the groups just never had a tradition of mobilizing. A lot of groups are discouraged.... I don't think it's an exaggeration to say they've been beaten down. People have really either been persuaded that it's [social change] just not going to happen, it [activism] just doesn't make any difference, it's a waste of our time, and so they're really demotivated, they just don't want to do it anymore. And I think there's an issue of real exhaustion in a lot of community groups. A lot of people are just spread so thin trying to do everything, or trying to do so much with so few resources, that there's kind of a general fatigue also. Last year there was a whole slew of people who left their jobs in the groups that we work with. For that variety of reasons I think: disillusionment, exhaustion, demotivation.

These are the key issues. If community organizations do not mobilize people and bring them into action, then what is their source of power? Mobilization of citizens acting for their own interests and building a powerful movement should still be the goal of community work. Without it, for those who want to see community organizations act as part of a wider movement for social change are frustrated and discouraged.

In Chapters 3 and 4, I traced the shift in the community sector from social activism towards service and development. However, this does not mean that there are no openings for renewal, especially as younger staff members are hired. Community organizations are still places where people who have little stake in the current political and economic system gather, and they can be used for education and mobilization, based on the tradition of support for social change activities. The change in perspective and consciousness of young activists is evident in those I interviewed. While they are committed to working in local struggles and projects, they are conscious of the local connection to the global picture. This consciousness is evident in their practice and the ideas that support it. Opposition to the global has to begin at the local and in specific mobilizations and projects that touch the lives of people in a direct way. This generation of activists and their leadership will help build a renewed and more politicized community movement with links to the past but with the potential to organize for social change.

CHAPTER SIX

TOWARDS A CONCLUSION: COMMUNITY ORGANIZING AND SOCIAL CHANGE

During the time I have been writing this book, I have renewed my involvement in community organizing and become more focussed on the world of practice. The book began as a critical reflection, coloured by pessimism about the contribution of community organizing practices to wider struggles for social justice and progressive social change. The problems and conditions that community organizations face on a daily basis are shaped by the inequalities of wealth and power and the relentless pressures of an unregulated marketplace to increase these inequities. Those in the community sector face difficult challenges as they balance the demands of people asking for help and services with those of funding bodies, while understanding that underlying all of these is the necessity for basic social change. However, influenced by those I interviewed and by a chance to involve myself in new forms of engagement, my perceptions have shifted, and I have become more optimistic about the future.

Today's activists and organizers, stimulated by the anti-globalization movement, articulate a political vision for their work, tying their practices directly to a process of social change. Whereas one of the biggest problems with the professionalization of organizing is the lack of commitment to mobilizing people in order to build a collective voice, those I interviewed believe that priority should be given to such mobilization and to taking action into the streets. For them, service provision, although present, is secondary and is linked to an educational agenda. They share an analysis of power in society—who has it and how it is used to maintain oppression. In addition, they have shifted away from the identity politics that dominated the 1980s and 1990s. Although most have a strong sense of personal identity shaped by gender, ethnicity, or disability, their organizing approaches and practices have gone beyond it to build common cause with many groups.

Identity politics begins with the individual and her/his specific group. For example, Irshad Manji's book *Risking Utopia: On the Edge of a New Democracy* (1997) opens with a discussion of who she is: a Moslem, a woman, and a lesbian. At the same time, she rejects the categories of feminism and socialism to describe her stance. The book parodies the left and travels down the road from identity politics to a politics of self in a world in which tolerance is the main challenge. Manji argues that identity has become so fragmented that the only category that remains is the individual and that we live in a society of individuals. Everything becomes relative in a world of trade-offs. She posits a society no longer shaped by interest and power, but one in which "nobody is 'given' justice. Everybody has the right and responsibility to bargain for it. To ensure that diversity is respected—a condition of belonging—patient negotiation must supplant instant gratification" (p. 139). In her world, as opposed to any kind of collective interest, the individual is the basic unit, and everything is negotiated from there. She states:

> my adaptation of radical democracy emphasizes the individual infinitely more than the institution.... That focus on the personal relationship is intentional. The age of institutions, from the family to the company, has died. In trying to update the concept of radical democracy, I treat it as a set of values that takes root with the individual and radiates out. (p. 155)

Identity politics has always played an ambiguous role. Many new groups have asserted their rights and demanded representation in the political sphere, insisting that their voices be heard. Beginning with the women's movement and followed by gays and lesbians, the disabled, and so on, these groups have challenged the orthodoxy of the traditional left and have created new opportunities for opposition. They made gains and in the process, contributed to a new politics of the left that was more inclusive, acknowledged difference, and created opportunities for new actors on the political scene.

In the period from the 1980s until recently, those working toward social change put a great deal of emphasis on identity as a way of revealing and reacting to conditions of oppression. Despite gains made, the emphasis on identity has acted to fragment opposition. As Andrea Levy (1994) argues:

> Identity politics represents not only the balkanization of the remnants of the left but also the abandonment of a larger vision or project of social transformation; taken to its logical extremes, the elevation of difference as the sole thing which defines us renders the idea of commonly held values on which such a vision can be based not only theoretically dubious but nefariously homogenizing. We appear to be on the verge of forgetting ... that commonality does not imply the obliteration of diversity, that the opposite pole of difference does not have to be sameness but solidarity. (p. 19)

Recognizing this, the people I interviewed have moved beyond identity politics and argue for a return to a broad opposition movement based on the common interest of those facing social and economic inequality. The women describe themselves as feminists. Those of minority ethnic or cultural communities understand their unique historical experiences and struggles but, at the same time, acknowledge their connection to others and to common experiences as the basis for a wider social and political solidarity. The challenge for this generation of organizers is, according to John Anner (1996):

> A reinvigorated social justice Movement with capital
> "M" will have to develop mechanisms of reconnecting
> identity politics with class issues, putting matters of
> economic justice on the front burner while showing
> how a racist and sexist power structure—now some-
> what more integrated—works to deny most people a
> decent life. (p. 11)

The interviews demonstrate that this challenge has been taken up
through a reinserting a broad political vision and the struggle for
basic social change within local organizing practice.

NEW PRACTICES

THE IMMIGRANT WORKERS' CENTRE

As I mentioned at the beginning of this chapter, I have become
involved again in several organizations that do contribute to processes
of social change. The Immigrant Workers' Centre (IWC) was
founded in 2000. (Two of the people I interviewed were key in its
development.) The idea for the centre grew out of the frustration of
two immigrant union organizers with the difficulties of organizing
immigrant workers and with the limits to conventional union
approaches. They believed that the actual workplace presented many
obstacles, such as intimidation by bosses, to bringing people together.
Further, in order for workplace struggle to succeed, broader support
was necessary, along with ongoing education and analysis. The IWC
acts primarily as a place for immigrants to Canada to meet and learn
about labour rights and to organize themselves on work-related questions. The community centre is a safe place to meet outside of work
and brings together workers of different backgrounds with union and
community activists. The IWC's program is formed by the issues
brought by workers coming into the centre, such as participation in a
campaign against the expulsion from Canada of a domestic live-in
caregiver and her son. The case received a lot of coverage and raised

not only the specific issues this woman faced but a critique of the wider situation of how immigrant labour is brought to Canada and the lack of rights in live-in conditions. Another campaign, launched in alliance with others, aims to improve the Labour Standards Act in Quebec. It grew out of the situation of several women who were laid off from a company and were unable to defend themselves because of large loopholes in the Act. In addition, the IWC has become a gathering place for many different groups, such as a Filipino youth group that is challenging the harassment many immigrant youth suffer at the hands of the police and lobbying for recreational and sports facilities to counter gang membership.

Organizationally, the IWC has a board and charter, but it functions more informally with a paid (badly and sometimes irregularly) coordinator and a loose, core group of activists. Specific working groups and campaigns have attracted both immigrant workers and allies, including student activists. Building an organizational structure is not given as high a priority as working directly on campaigns, education, and mobilization. The practice of the IWC contrasts significantly with the majority of service and development organizations. It is explicitly political in the sense that its leadership understands its work as linking local struggles to global concerns and other international social movements and as making sure that political education is always present. Further, building a bridge between workplace and community organizing has always been a huge challenge for both unions and the community. The different cultures and styles of organizing are not easy to overcome. However, several unions have given financial and other support to the IWC and have collaborated with it on specific activities.

The IWC is firmly in the social action tradition, fighting on labour issues through mobilizing people and their allies. Because it is a relatively young organization and because it does not fall into traditional categories, it has not received funding from government agencies that support community organizations. With its support from unions, it has been able to carry out its activities without having to compromise its mission or orientation. However, the IWC is financially unstable and has had to live with a very limited budget.

This seems to be the new reality for groups that do not fall into government-defined service and development categories. The IWC combines intervention on the specific issues of immigrant workers with a broader socio-political analysis and mobilization for social justice. In addition, it has made connections between local and global action, establishing links with a new generation of activists in the struggle against corporate power.

ECO-INITIATIVES

Eco-Initiatives is an organization in my neighbourhood that promotes urban agriculture. It comes out of an ecological tradition and combines community development with collective gardens. The gardens are a place for residents to meet and work collectively to produce fresh organic produce for themselves and for local organizations that provide food for low-income people. It began as part of a municipal recycling program; its role was to educate and to encourage participation in the program. Because of increased bureaucratic pressures and controls exerted by the city, the organization decided to break from this relationship and pursue only the urban agriculture agenda. As a consequence, it is financially less stable, but more autonomous in pursuit of its goals. It is also involved in a wider network of organizations that examines the issue of food security.

Eco-Initiatives practice can be described as within the community development approach. It does not engage in action strategies nor mobilize people to make demands for social change. Its politics are carried out in different ways. The gardens are a place of social solidarity where people gather to produce food in a way that is different from the one dominated by corporations. In one of the interviews in Chapter 5, a young woman employed there talks about community gardens as a place for political education. Since the gardens are not individual plots but collective, they encourage a culture in which direct participation in a collective is an important objective. Politics are expressed through the understanding that organic urban agriculture opposes corporate-dominated food production and distribution and creates an alternative to it. In this aspect, Eco-initiatives is part of a movement that preserves heritage seeds discarded by mass production. For example, a variety of melons known as Montreal Melons had disappeared. Eco-Initiatives workers tracked down the seeds from a small producer in the United States and reintroduced this melon to its own gardens as well as selling the seeds to private gardens. An ecological consciousness is promoted through these types of activities. Further, community gardens belong in the movement toward more sustainable neighbourhoods, which redefines what functions can be carried out locally and contributes toward greater collective self-reliance. Creating alternatives to capitalism through even small activities like the gardens contributes to building a new political and social culture at the local level.

THE POPULAR ARCHIVES OF POINTE ST. CHARLES

The third organization with which I have become involved was founded in order to keep alive the traditions of community organization practice. The Popular Archives of Pointe St. Charles is located in a working-class neighbourhood with a long history of militant community organizing and alternative organizations. It was the birthplace of the first CED organizations in Montreal, community health and legal clinics. Many organizations have worked in the struggle against poverty in the area, providing services and education, and these groups continue to mobilize locally. In addition, the residents have mobilized effectively to defend their clinics against government attempts to take them over or close them. The ratio of French-speakers to English-speakers is 60 to 40; both groups have their own organizations and histories and have worked together in major struggles. Because of the high percentage of social housing—non-profits, cooperatives, and public—the community has limited the pressures of gentrification. As a consequence, many older activists have remained, and there are some new projects created by younger residents. At the same time, because no one organization has systematically gathered the traditions together, there has been a loss of the history of these organizing efforts. Documents, photos, and videotapes of these earlier periods are decaying, unsorted, and stored in basements. One goal of the Popular

Archive is to reclaim these materials; another is to use these materials for popular education, linking past traditions to present struggles.

The Popular Archive has created a video and film festival, featuring more than 40 videos and films made on community life and organizing. An after-school program introduces young children to community organizations and their history. A large exhibit on the role of women in the community and how this role has changed over the last 50 years was prepared for the World March of Women in 2000. Interviews with women active in the community were used to construct the exhibit. Following its success and the demand in both the local and wider community for its display, a wider project celebrating the contribution of women to the development of community organizing was initiated under the leadership of a Ph.D. student. Entitled "Tissons une courte pointe: L'histoire de l'action communautaire à travers les histoires de vies de femmes de Pointe-St-Charles" (Weaving a quilt: History of community action via the life stories of women from Point St. Charles), this project was made up of two groups of women, one French and the other English-speaking. All of the women had participated in a variety of ways in the neighbourhood and shared not only their stories but also the impact of their participation on their lives. Out of this project came the production of a book and video. In the long-term, an inter-generation project is planned.

The board of the Archives is small with the leadership coming from people who have been leading activists in the community over more than 25 years. The idea of the archive is to promote a consciousness of struggle and opposition within the area and to celebrate these traditions—to make history real and link it to present struggles. It is easy for history to disappear with the loss of documents and the death or disengagement of older activists and organizers. Connecting generations provides continuity and gives those involved in the daily struggles support and insights.

As with the other two organizations, the Popular Archives faces a difficult time financially. The Quebec government's funding programs specify sectoral categories. Organizations that fall outside of these categories have trouble receiving support. The Archive is perceived neither as a formal archive nor as a specialist in popular education. Therefore, the main source of its support has come from a foundation, but this is time-limited. The lack of a proper funding base has created internal stress and has limited the potential of the organization to expand its archiving and educational activities. I describe the archive because it is an example of how the traditions of a district have been preserved. In Chapters 3 and 4 two approaches to community organizing were discussed—action and development. I argued there that the political and economic context and external pressures have contributed to the shaping or recasting of practice. With the restructuring of the 1980s, many of the older action traditions were abandoned for moderation, partnerships, and development. Pointe St. Charles was also subjected to these pressures, and its CED organization has gone that route. However, the tradition of mobilization and action is still alive and well. The Archives supports this tradition and contributes to this continuity.

These three examples contribute to a process of social change. They do so in different ways, linking action and education and a vision of community as a place for the mobilization of political struggles and the creation of social alternatives. A couple of lessons come out of these experiences. First, social change is not necessarily linked to a particular model of practice. Second, organizations that bring people together and that provide activities connected to their daily lives and linked to broader political questions and traditions can be the basis for building local activism and for wider movements for social change.

TOWARDS A CONCLUSION: REVISITING COMMUNITY ORGANIZING MODELS

Each of these three organizations has within its practice and wider orientation elements of a struggle for basic social change. Although the practices can also be viewed as constrained by the system, the tension lived in these organizations is between performing specific activities that are within the boundaries and simultaneously working beyond those limits. The tension—and how organizations and organizers work with it—is the key dilemma.

In Chapter 2, I cited the work of Rothman (1999) and Minkler and Wallerstein (1999) to examine the action and development models or approaches. Here, I will revisit them with a priority given to the question of social change as the starting point in exploring a different approach to community organizing practice.[1] The action and development models and the literature concerning them examine practice elements and strategies. The politics tends to be limited to what can be described as "pragmatic reformism," that is, improving social conditions within the boundaries of what exits. I have raised the question of how community organizing can move beyond this and contribute to basic social change. The issue is complex; it is not easy to separate limited gains from long-term social change because engagement in the "real world" inevitably leads to pushing for specific victories. The difference between those practices that are limited to specific gains only and those that see practice as part of a process of wider social change is due to factors such as intention, vision, process, and alliances. Both action and development can contribute to social change or can play a role in maintaining the status quo by not moving beyond specific local gains; both can also have a lasting impact by changing the consciousness of the groups they serve, thus creating conditions for mobilization for social and political change.

The table below expresses the relationship between the development and action approaches and the question of social change. I have used the terms integration and opposition in order to contrast the politics of practice. Integration strategies are used to increase people's participation in the system as it is or to enlarge resources or distribute some goods a little more fairly without challenging the basic assumptions of the system itself. This can happen either through pressure group tactics or through a variety of social programs. For example, local organizing to pressure the municipal government to improve traffic patterns or garbage pick-up can better the quality of life in a neighbourhood but does not challenge the domination of the

---

[1] Thanks to Bob Fisher, Marie Lacroix, and a workshop on issues in Community Economic Development for suffering through attempts at developing this work and for their respective insights.

car or the patterns of waste production. Similarly, programs such as job readiness attempt to place people in the labour market but do not necessarily raise questions about working conditions or about the pattern of linking jobs to participation in consumer culture. Integration practices support the maintenance of the fundamental power relations of our society and are designed to help people either meet their needs or make gains within existing structures and processes They assume that the system can expand to accommodate and bring people into either the jobs or the life-styles defined by corporate capitalism. They do not question the limits and competitive nature of the system. Organizing within this approach does not go beyond either the limitation of local, winnable demands or service and development.

In contrast, those working on the opposition side understand local organizing as part of a process of fundamental social change. This can include both organizing opposition to different aspects of society, such as specific policy or forms of oppression and inequality, and creating local alternatives such as cooperatives and services. These practices challenge the basic relations of power and create an alternative political and social culture based on democracy and direct control by citizens of these organizations. Further, the process of reaching these ends is through mobilizing citizens to play an active role. This is a key element, and the one aspect of practice that has been reduced since the 1980s. Power relations can be challenged and shifted only through the collective actions of citizens. Community organizing, to be a force for social change, has to be able to mobilize locally but must act in conjunction with wider alliances that share a politics of opposition.

The differences are not always clear-cut and it is hard to classify actual day-to-day practices. It is for that reason that I have added the middle column—overlapping practices—to the table. In some respects, the actual activities are less important than the processes around them. This means, for example, that specific demands, campaigns, or services at the local level are integral to community organizing and fall within a process of building opposition. The process of organizing is what is important, not just the outcome. This includes raising critical consciousness in those participating in the organizing process about the necessity of social transformation as the means to achieve social justice and democracy. In addition, local work must be connected to broader social movements and coalitions that are part of a struggle for social change. Gutierrez and Lewis (1995), for instance, understand specific activities by feminist organizers at the local level as tied to the broader social movement.

The table illustrates the dimensions of integration/opposition along with the action/development approaches. I have included traditions in order to illustrate each approach.

	INTEGRATION	OVERLAPPING PRACTICES	OPPOSITION
DEVELOPMENT	Service provision and development schemes based on professional leadership and a consensus model.	Service provision at the local level.	Building alternatives that create new democratic or non-market economics, new practices that are "pre-figurative."
	Tradition: Asset/capacity building (e.g., McKnight).		Tradition: Feminist services or green urban development (e.g., collective community gardens).
ACTION	Pluralist pressure group organizing Tradition: Pluralist pressure groups (e.g., Alinsky).	Organizing people in a neighbourhood to pressure for local improvements.	Social movement organizing and critical consciousness, challenging the legitimacy of existing power relations. Tradition: Social movement organizing locally (e.g., anti-globalization activism).

Integration/Development is currently the dominant approach. It includes the community development described in Chapter 4, which is defined by social partnerships, supporting civil society organizations, and consensus-oriented strategies such as asset/capacity-building. Change is understood as an internally defined local process, and solutions to social and economic problems are sought within what already exists in the community, although outside resources may be required. Local democracy through participation of citizens is a factor, but the focus is limited to local improvement with an underlying assumption that self-help is a primary element. Integration/Action is primarily a pressure group approach, which assumes political pluralism in the wider society. The goal of the organizing is to gain local improvements by applying pressure on those with authority to bring about changes. This approach also focusses on the local, although it includes alliances with others with common interests. Some of the organizations operating under this practice have a longer view of building power, but it is within the boundaries of local improvement. Often "radical" or disruptive tactics obscure the more traditional goals that these tactics are used to reach. In both of the Integrative quadrants, there are elements of practice that contribute to wider social change, but this is not their primary focus (this was discussed at the end of Chapter 4). Rather, it is an unintended consequence that comes from people working together for social improvement and beginning to build solidarity and a critical analysis. It is this blurring that creates the overlapping categories on the chart.

Both quadrants under opposition contain practices and organizations that advance wider processes of social change. They go beyond the immediate goals and specific practices shared, at times, with those of an integrative orientation because of a self-conscious commitment to intention and vision. Intention implies an understanding of what the organization is trying to do and naming it. Kovel (2002), in his book on eco-socialism, argues that intentional communities and intentionality can be understood as material forces. He says, "the generation of some kind of collective 'intentions' that can withstand the power of capital's force field will be necessary for creating an eco-socialist society" (p. 194). Naming the essence of our work is the key aspect, although there are risks involved. What will the implications be for the sources of support? Will it upset "partners"? There is a difficult line between pragmatism shaped by the demands of others and an understanding of the goals of social change. There must be an adequate number of people working together who share these directions, rather than a small group of conspirators within the staff of an organization. Community organizations *can* contribute to the building of a wider oppositional culture. In order for that to happen, the analysis and alternative direction has to be articulated in a clear vision. Vision is naming the long-term objectives of the organizing process and how they connect to the type of society we would like to see. It incorporates the core values of the organization and relates these to its long-term goals and direction, along with defining strategies of how to get there. The vision orients the politics of the organization and helps sustains the direction over time. Gindin (2002) describes vision in the context of the resistance to corporate globalization:

> Social justice demands reviving the determination to dream. It is not just that dreaming is essential for maintaining any resistance, but because today, if we do not think big—as big as the globalizers themselves think—we will not even win small. (p. 2)

This level of vision implies that the community movement has to see itself in fundamental opposition to the basic relations of power and domination in our society and must look toward a future in which all forms of hierarchy and domination are ended. This is a monumental task, and it is only in alliance with others that there is even a remote possibility that it can happen. More importantly, without a vision of what is basic and how this connects to the short term and its related process, it is impossible to get beyond the demands of service or limited campaigns. This does not mean that the vision has to be rigid, but it should act to orient both practice goals and processes. Day-to-day local work requires pragmatic engagement with pressures from funders and working for specific objectives; as a result, long-term goals can be forgotten or ignored. One reason for maintaining and articulating vision is to balance specific short-term demands with long-term values and social change objectives. Differentiating between mandate and vision permits a naming of the long- and short-term aspects of an organization. Specific mandates should be shaped by the wider vision. In other words, it is important that organizations do not restrict their definition of vision to their particular activities. One way of doing this is to emphasize process and alliances.

The Opposition/Action quadrant includes those social action organizations that intentionally work beyond the local. For example, the student left of the 1960s and 1970s was involved in establishing welfare rights and grassroots neighbourhood organizations. These mobilized people, contested policies of government, and demanded social rights for the poor. Similarly, as mentioned earlier, the women's movement put in place new services that recognized needs and redefined social issues from the point of view of women. Many of these organizations continue to exist, and, although they may be less politically engaged nowadays, they are nonetheless present in social struggles. Social movements, by definition, have a short life. They rise into prominence and then decline. Organizations founded by movement activists provide continuity despite the transformations they go through, such as service development and the replacement of activists by professionals whose practice is to represent those they serve rather than to mobilize them. The initial values and visions do not entirely disappear. As new movements arise or campaigns are launched, community-based organizations play a role in supporting and nourishing them and offer a place from which to mobilize and carry out political education. The IWC is an organization of the Opposition/Action type. Its vision goes beyond specific campaigns such as labour code reforms and rights agenda. It has informal links with anti-globalization activists, participates in a variety of ways with them in demonstrations and other activities, and mobilizes for common actions. It also has connections to international bodies concerned about issues facing migrant workers. Seeing itself as part of an international struggle against exploitation of migrant and other workers, its programs of education aim to draw together immediate problems with a deeper analysis of the wider political and economic context. Many of those interviewed in Chapter 5 see their engagement in a similar way; that is, they combine basic social transformation with specific practices.

Opposition/Development couples services and/or development to the process of social change to create alternatives to the present system as either places free from hierarchies or as models of a different type of society. The organizations with this orientation are democratic and participate in a wider culture of opposition. For example, service organizations that grew out of social movements maintain a commitment to social change work. Two examples illustrate this point. The feminist movement in the 1970s created services such as rape crisis centres and shelters for victims of domestic abuse, but these were contextualized in campaigns for public recognition of these issues. Women mobilized to demand public support for these services. The services themselves were often run by collectives and concentrated not only on providing safe spaces but also on raising the consciousness both of the users of their services and the wider community. Similarly, community clinics, democratically controlled by residents and employees, combined health services with education and popular mobilization on a variety of issues. The Pointe St. Charles Community Clinic continues to employ community organizers who mobilize and educate the public on many different social issues.

There is another tradition that falls within this quadrant. Economic alternatives, in which ownership is collective rather than individual, remove production of goods and service from the market and prioritize need rather than profit as the reason for production. The creation of "green alternatives," such as Eco-Initiatives, is part of this orientation. Morrison's (1995) vision of "ecological democracy" requires the growth of democratic and community-based alternatives. These encompass both human services and other activities. He argues that these associations are "the basic venue for moving power away from state and corporate bureaucracies" (p. 139). The creation of alternatives has to move beyond local work to federated structures that build an "associative democracy" that acts to transfer power from government and market to community. Similarly, Kovel (2002) sees local associations as:

> prefigurative praxes that are to overcome capital in an ecosocialist way are at once remote and exactly at hand. They are remote insofar as the entire regime of capital stands in the way of their realization, and they are at hand insofar as the movement toward the future exists embedded in every point of social organism where a need arises. (p. 217)

Perhaps Kovel overstates the case, but the tradition of creating social alternatives to either the state or capital is a long one, rooted particularly in anarchist traditions. Such organizations play several roles, including demonstrating that people without managers can create forms of local production and services.

Both action and development organizations committed to social change have an impact on the daily lives of citizens, thus encouraging their participation in social change activities. These processes have the potential of helping community organizations move beyond their specific goals and day-to-day activities to create a culture of opposition. As I discussed earlier, community organizations, particularly those founded since the 1960s, grew out of a tradition of direct and/or participatory democracy, creating places in which citizens can have a role in shaping their own lives and local community. As power in our society becomes increasingly remote, activities that are controlled by citizens become more important; open discussion and debate lead to participation in decision-making processes and give people a voice on wider issues. This reduces the passivity generated by a consumer society in which the only real decision people are asked to make is which brand-named product meets their manipulated desires and wants. Real politics is neither about consumerism nor electoral choices every four or five years but about active participation in society where citizens can represent their own interests and create alternatives. Community organizations offer this opportunity.

Community and popular education are important tools in building leadership and local power. Lotz (1997) traces the history of education, community development, and organizing practice as far back as the emergence of university extension departments in 1914 in Alberta. The most developed and long-lasting of these efforts was the "Antigonish movement," pioneered in the 1920s in Nova Scotia by Fathers Jimmy Tompkins and Michael Coady. Responding to the poverty of local fishing and mining communities, they educated workers for action, building new institutions such as credit unions and cooperatives to improve social and economic conditions. According to Lotz (1997):

> By the end of 1931, 173 study clubs had been estab-
> lished, most of them in rural Scottish Catholic
> parishes.... By 1939, the movement had established 342
> credit unions and 162 other forms of cooperative organ-
> izations. The Antigonish approach was summarized in
> four imperatives: Listen! Study! Discuss! Act! (p. 21)

Education within community organizations can be formal sessions
or informal learning situations. In either case, people develop an
analysis of interest and power and come to understand the political
and social stake they have in the larger society. The lessons can be
local and related to organizational self-interest, but underlying these
are issues of power, how it operates and how to challenge it. The
process demystifies the notion that the political system operates for all
of us and helps people learn how to make demands that promote their
rights and specific interests. Brandt (2002) describes it as follows:

> Popular education ... aims to unveil, analyze and trans-
> form power relations, based on class, race/ethnicity,
> gender, sexuality, age, religion, or any social dimension
> of oppression. It promotes democratic practice
> through teaching/learning processes that are collec-
> tive, critical, systematic, participatory, and creative.
> Motivated by principles of equality and justice, it inte-
> grates research, learning, and organizing for social
> change. (p. 68)

It is important that local issues and actions provide opportunities
both for making specific changes in such a way that the people
involved gain a sense of power through collective action and for connecting to wider movements and deepening a critical analysis of how
power is structured and how it operates.

Many community organizations have been effective in building
local power and having influence at that level. This is both a strength
and an opportunity, but it has its limits. Community organizations
participate in local "tables," or groups of organizations, based on

neighbourhoods and/or sectors sharing a common interest. As a result, some degree of local power can be mobilized. There are two weaknesses, however. First, often the main purpose of these "tables" is to negotiate support for the organizations from the government; organizational self-interest shapes the way that they "do business." Second, since the vision of these bodies is limited, either because of locality or sectoral interests, it is difficult for them to go beyond these concerns and engage in broad political and social struggles. However, even with these limits, these bodies have been significant in their participation in campaigns and wider social mobilizations, such as the World March of Women in 2000, discussed earlier. Social movements in general need to see these community-based organizations, even moderate ones, as potential allies who can be brought into action under certain conditions.

Community organizations carry progressive values into practice. Despite all the pressures on them to collapse into some kind of politically innocuous service entity, many have managed to use the resources from the state and/or private foundations to contribute to ongoing political education and mobilization for citizens to struggle for social and economic justice. It is not easy to balance the demands of those funding these organizations with the traditions of social change and wider activism. The three groups briefly presented in this chapter illustrate the financial consequences of promoting social change and community alternatives in terms that are not compromised. Mobilization of citizens for action, education, and agitation, within the democratic process, is the most important work of these organizations. Those that create economic and social alternatives embody progressive values; however, they do not create a new society within the shell of capitalism but do provide a meeting place and a small alternative economy. We need to mobilize for action, but we also need alternatives so we can live our values. As Michael Albert (2002) states:

> We chose issues to better the lot of suffering constituencies and to simultaneously increase prospects for more gains in the future. Short term, we raise social costs until elites begin to implement our demands or

end policies that we oppose. Longer term, we accumu-
late support and develop movement infrastructure and
alternative institutions, while working toward transforming society's defining relations. (p. x)

Building opposition is thus two-pronged. One dimension is
action that transcends the local; the other builds democratic alternatives. Both provide opportunities for political education and contribute to a culture of opposition. Most of the leadership of the community movement from the late 1970s has had a socialist vision of
some kind and has understood the limits of capitalism. In our present period, we are taught to believe that "There Is No Alternative"
(TINA). We have to rethink some of the older doctrines, but we
must name the problem—global capitalism—and renew our vision of
the type of future we want and how we see getting there. This is the
starting point for renewal.

This book has looked backwards at the contradictory traditions of
community organizing and has looked ahead to what might be the
future with a renewed commitment to fundamental social change. In
acknowledging all the pressures to move practice towards integration, we cannot lose sight of why many of us got into the field. We
wanted to do more than "do good," which will always be inadequate
in a world that has given more and more power and wealth to the few
and impoverishes the many. Doing good maintains these relations
and allows social inequalities, social problems, and environmental
destruction to grow.

Anger is an appropriate response to injustice; we tend to forget
our anger, as the community sector has become more sophisticated
and is accepted as an important social actor and as we become
"strategic" and "professional." Kathryn Addelson (1991) speaks of
her own experience and that of others:

I grew up angry.... Angry because my people, my
neighbors, my family were defeated by a sense of pow-
erlessness.... [Consider the] lives of people who grew
up angry. If these people are different from other

people, it's because they learned what to do with their anger. They learned how to begin to change things. They learned how to turn their anger outward and make it creative.... Our growing up angry was not unusual. Revolutionaries are not adventurers. They come out of ordinary lives and want to make a revolution to change ordinary lives. (p. 4)

Community organizing for social change begins with this impulse. Learning what to do with our anger and outrage, bringing it to local struggles, broadening and extending it, and keeping it to fuel our drive for social justice: this is the challenge.

REFERENCES

Adamson, N., Briskin, L., McPhail, M. (1988). *Feminist organizing for change: The contemporary women's movement in Canada*. Toronto, ON: Oxford University Press.

Addelson, K. (1991). *Impure thoughts: Essays on philosophy, feminism and ethics*. Philadelphia, PA: Temple University Press.

Albert, M. (2002). *The trajectory of change: Activist strategies for social transformation*. Cambridge, MA: South End Press.

Albert, M., Cagan, L., Chomsky, N., Hahnel, R., King, M., Sargent, L., and Sklar, H. (1986). *Liberating theory*. Cambridge, MA: South End Press.

Alinsky, Saul D. (1971). *Rules for radicals: A pragmatic primer for realistic radicals*. New York, NY: Vintage Books.

Anner, J. (Ed.). (1996). *Beyond identity politics: Emerging social justice movements in communities of color*. Boston, MA: South End Press.

Arnopoulos, S. (1970). Two days without sleep: Welfare protesters still have no answer. *The Montreal Daily Star* (July 16): 21.

Barker, J. (1999). *Street level democracy: Political settings at the margins of global power*. Toronto, ON: Between the Lines.

Benello, G. (1972). Social animation among anglophone groups in Québec. In F. Lesemann and M. Thienot (Eds.), *Animations sociales au Québec* (pp. 435–94). Montreal, QC: Ecole de Service Social, Université de Montréal.

Brandt, B. (2002). *Tangled routes: Women, work, and globalization on the tomato trail.* Aurora, ON: Garamond.

Breines, W. (1989). *Community and organization in the New Left, 1962–1968: The great refusal.* New Brunswick, NJ: Rutgers University Press.

Briskin, L. (1991). Feminist practice: A new approach to evaluating feminist strategy. In J.D. Wine and J.L. Ristock (Eds.), *Women and social change: Feminist activism in Canada* (pp. 24–40). Toronto, ON: Lorimer.

Brodhead, D., Goodings, S., and Brodhead, M. (1997). The Company of Young Canadians. In B. Wharf and M. Clague (Eds.), *Community organizing: Canadian experiences* (pp. 137–48). Toronto, ON: Oxford University Press.

Browne, P.L. (2001). Rethinking globalization, class and the state. *Canadian Review of Social Policy* 48 (Fall): 93–102.

Bruyn, S.T. (1987). Beyond the market and the state. In S.T. Bruyn and J. Meehan (Eds.). *Beyond the state and the market: New directions in community development* (pp. 3–27). Philadelphia, PA: Temple University Press.

Bruyn, S.T., and Meehan, J. (Eds.). (1987). *Beyond the state and the market: New directions in community development.* Philadelphia, PA: Temple University Press.

Callahan, M. (1997). Feminist community organizing in Canada: Postcards from the edge. In B. Wharf and M. Clague (Eds.), *Community organizing: Canadian experiences* (pp. 181–204). Toronto, ON: Oxford University Press.

Cervero, R., and Wilson, A. (2001). At the heart of practice: The struggle for knowledge and power." In R. Cervero, A. Wilson, and Associates (Eds.), *Power in practice: Adult education for knowledge and power in society* (pp. 1–21). San Francisco, CA: Jossey-Bass.

Chaskin, R.J., Joseph, M.L., and Chipenda-Dansokho, S. (1998). Implementing comprehensive community development: Possibilities and limitations. In P. Ewalt, E. Freeman, and D. Poole (Eds.), *Community building: Renewal, well being and shared responsibility* (pp. 17–28). Washington, DC: NASW Press.

Chic Resto-Pop. (1995). *Déclaration des travailleurs et travailleuses exclus.* Montreal: n.p. (3 novembre).

Church, K. (1997). Business (not quite) as usual: Psychiatric survivors and community economic development in Ontario. In E. Shragge (Ed.). *Community economic development: In search of empowerment* (pp. 48–71). Montreal, QC: Black Rose Books.

Church, K., Fontan, J-M., Ng, R., and Shragge, E. (2000). *Social learning among those who are excluded from the labour market. Part One: Context and case studies.* Toronto, ON: Network for New Approaches to Lifelong Learning, Ontario Institute for Studies in Education.

Clague, M., and Wharf, B. (Eds.), *Community organizing: Canadian experiences.* Toronto, ON: Oxford University Press.

Clarke, S.E., and Gaile, G.L. (1998). *The work of cities.* Minneapolis, MN: University of Minnesota Press.

Cloward, R.A., and Piven, F.F. (1977). *Poor people's movements: Why they succeed and how they fail.* New York, NY: Pantheon Books.

Cloward, R.A., and Piven, F.F. (1999). Disruptive dissensus: People and power in the industrial age. In J. Rothman (Ed.), *Reflections on community organization: Enduring themes and critical issues* (pp. 165–93). Itasca, IL: F.E. Peacock.

Daly, M. (1970). *The revolution game.* Toronto, ON: New Press.

DeRoche, C.P. (1998). Through a glass darkly: Looking for CED. In G.A. MacIntyre (Ed.), *Perspectives on communities: A community economic development roundtable* (pp. 201–24). Sydney, NS: University College of Cape Breton.

Doucet, L., and Favreau, L. (1991). L'organization communautaire de 1960 à aujourd'hui. In L. Doucet et L. Favreau, *Théorie et pratiques en organisation communautaire* (pp. 35–56). Québec City, QC: Presses de l'Université du Québec.

Drover,G., and Shragge, E. (1979). Urban struggle and organizing strategies. *Our Generation* 13, 1: 61–76.

Evans, S. and Boyte, H. (1992). *Free spaces: The sources of democratic change in America.* 2nd ed. Chicago, IL: University of Chicago Press.

Ewalt, P., Freeman, E., and Poole, D. (Eds.). (1998). *Community building: Renewal, well being and shared responsibility*. Washington, DC: NASW Press.

Ewalt, P. (1998). The revitalization of impoverished communities. In P. Ewalt et al. (Eds.), *Community building: Renewal, well being and shared responsibility* (pp. 3–5). Washington, DC: NASW Press.

Favreau, L. (1989). *Mouvement populaire et intervention communautaire de 1960 a nos jours, continuités et Ruptures*. Montréal, QC: Centre de Formation Populaire et Les Editions du Fleuve.

Ferrante, A. (1972). Family allowance proposal: Welfare hikes held up until accord "a reality." *The Montreal Daily Star* (February 8): 3.

Fisher, R. (1994). *Let the people decide: Neighborhood organizing in America*. Rev.ed. New York, NY: Twayne Publishers.

Fisher, R. (1999). The importance of history and context in community crganization. In J. Rothman (Ed.), *Reflections on community organization: Enduring themes and critical issues* (pp. 335–53). Itasca, IL: F.E. Peacock.

Fisher, R. (2001). Political economy and public life: The context for community organizing. In J. Rothman, J.L. Erlich, and J.E. Tropman (Eds.), *Strategies of community intervention*. 6th ed. (pp. 100–17). Itasca, IL: F.E. Peacock.

Fisher, R., and Shragge, E. (2000). Challenging community organizing: Facing the 21st century. *Journal of Community Practice* 8, 3: 1–20.

Foley, G. (1999). *Learning in social action: A contribution to understanding informal education*. London and New York, NY: Zed Books.

Fontan, J-M. (1988). Development economique communautaire à Montréal. *Possibles* 12, 2 (printemps): 12–23.

Fontan, J-M. (1993). *A critical review of Canadian, American, and European Community economic development literature*. Vancouver, BC: CCE/Westcoast Publications.

Fontan, J-M. (1994). Le Développement économique communautaire québecois: éléments de synthèse et point de vue critique. *Liens social et politiques—RIAC* 32 (automne): 115–26.

Fontan, J-M., and Shragge, E. (1996). Chic Resto-Pop: New community practice in Quebec. *Community Development Journal: An International Forum* 31, 4: 291–301.

Fontan, J-M., and Shragge, E. (1998). Community economic development organizations in Montreal. *Journal of Community Practice* 5, 1/2: 125–36.

Frank, F., and Smith, A. (1999). *The community development handbook: A tool to build community capacity.* Ottawa, ON: Human Resources Development Canada.

Gindin, S. (2002). Social justice and globalization. *Monthly Review* 54, 2: 1–11.

GMAPCC. (1972). *Statement of principles for the Greater Montreal Anti-Poverty.* Unpublished document. Greater Montreal Anti-Poverty Coordinating Committee.

Gutierrez, L.M., and Lewis, E. (1995). A feminist perspective on organizing with women of color. In F.G. Rivera and J.L. Erlich (Eds.), *Community organizing in a diverse society.* 2nd ed. (pp. 95–112). Boston, MA: Allyn and Bacon.

Hamel, P., and Léonard, J-F. (1980). Ambivalence des luttes urbaines et ambiguïté des intervention de l'état. *Revue Internationale d'Action Communautaire* 4, 44 (automne): 74–82.

Hasson, S., and Ley, D. (1994). *Neighbourhood organizations and the welfare state.* Toronto, ON: University of Toronto Press.

Hayden, T. (1988). *Reunion: A memoir.* New York, NY: Collier Books.

Homan, M. (1999). *Promoting community change: Making it happen in the real world.* 2nd ed. Pacific Grove, CA: Brooks Cole Publishing Company.

In and against the state. (1979). London/Edinburgh Weekend Return Group. N.p.

Keck, J., and Fulks, W. (1997). Meaningful work and community betterment: The case of Opportunities for Youth and Local Initiatives Program (1971–1973). In B. Wharf and M. Clague (Eds.), *Community organizing: Canadian experiences* (pp. 113–36). Toronto, ON: Oxford University Press.

Klein, N. (2000). *No logo: Taking aim at the brand bullies.* Toronto, ON: Knopf.

Kovel, J. (2002). *The enemy of nature: The end of capitalism or the end of the world?* Halifax, NS: Fernwood Press and London: Zed Press.

Kretzmann, J., and McKnight, J. (1993). *Building communities from the inside out: A path toward finding and mobilizing a community's assets.* Chicago, IL: Acta Publications.

Kruzynski, A., and Shragge, E. (1999). Getting organized: Anti-poverty organizing and social citizenship in the 1970s. *Community Development Journal: An International Forum* 34, 4 (October): 328–39.

Laxer, J. (1996). *In search of a New Left: Canadian politics after the neo-conservative assault.* Toronto, ON: Viking Press.

Lemert, C. (1993). *Social theory: The multicultural and classic readings.* Boulder, CO: Westview Press.

Levy, A. (1994). Progeny and progress? Reflections on the legacy of the New Left. *Our Generation* 24, 2: 1–38.

Lotz, J. (1997). The beginning of community development in English-speaking Canada. In B. Wharf and M. Clague (Eds.), *Community organizing: Canadian experiences* (pp. 15–28). Toronto, ON: Oxford University Press.

Lotz, J. (1998). *The lichen factor: The quest for community development in Canada.* Sydney, NS: University College of Cape Breton Press.

Lustiger-Thaler, H., and Shragge, E. (1993). Social movements and social welfare: The political problem of needs. In G. Drover and P. Kearns (Eds.). *New approaches to welfare theory* (pp. 161–76). Aldershot, England: Edward Elgar.

Manji, I. (1997). *Risking utopia: On the edge of a new democracy.* Toronto, ON and Vancouver, BC: Douglas and McIntyre.

McGrath, S., Moffat, K., and George, U. (1999). Community capacity: The emperor's new clothes. *Canadian Review of Social Policy* 44: 9–23.

McKnight, J. (1995A). Asset-based community building. *City Magazine* 16, 2 (Summer): 10–12.

McKnight, J. (1995B). *The careless society: Community and its counterfeits.* New York, NY: Basic Books.

McKnight, J.L., and Kretzmann, J.P. (1999). Mapping community capacity. In M. Minkler (Ed.), *Community organizing and community building for health* (pp. 157–72). New Brunswick, NJ: Rutgers University Press.

Miller, J. (1987). *Democracy in the streets: Form Port Huron to the siege of Chicago.* New York, NY: Simon and Schuster.

Minkler, M., and Wallerstein, N. (1999). Improving health through community organization and community building: A health education perspective. In M. Minkler (Ed.), *Community organizing and community building for health* (pp. 30–52). New Brunswick, NJ: Rutgers University Press.

Mondros, J., and Wilson, S.M. (1994). *Organizing for power and empowerment.* New York, NY: Columbia University Press.

Morris, D. (1996). Communities: Building authority, responsibility, and capacity. In J. Mander and E. Goldsmith (Eds), *The case against the global economy and for a turn toward the local* (pp. 434–45). San Francisco, CA: Sierra Club.

Morrison, R. (1995). *Ecological democracy.* Boston, MA: South End Press.

Murphy, B. (1999). *Transforming ourselves, transforming the world: An open conspiracy for social change.* Halifax, NS: Fernwood; London: Zed Press; Ottawa, ON: InterPares.

Naparstek, A.J., and Dooley, D. (1998). Countering urban disinvestment through community-building initiatives. In P. Ewalt et al. (Eds.), *Community building: renewal, well being and shared responsibility* (pp. 6–16). Washington, DC: NASW Press.

Ninacs, W. (1997). Entraide économique, création d'entrprises, politiques sociales et "empowerment." *Nouvelles practiques sociales* 8, 1: 97–119.

Our Generation. (1969). Editorial: Towards an extra-parliamentary opposition in Canada. *Our Generation* 6, 4: 3–19.

Panet-Raymond, J. (1987). Community groups in Québec: From radical action to voluntarism for the state. *Community Development Journal* 22, 4: 281–86.

Panet-Raymond, J. (1992). Partnership: Myth or reality? *Community Development Journal* 27, 2 (April): 156–65.

Panet-Raymond, J. and Mayer, R. (1997). The history of community development in Quebec. In B. Wharf and M. Clague (Eds.), *Community organizing: Canadian experiences* (pp. 29–61). Toronto, ON: Oxford University Press.

PERM (Pointe St. Charles Equal Rights Movement). (1971).
Videotape. Montreal: Parallel Institute.

Popple, K. (1995). *Analysing community work: Its theory and practice.*
Bristol, England: Open University Press.

Putnam, R.D. (1995) "Bowling alone": America's declining social
capital. *Journal of Democracy* 6, 1 (January): 65–78.

Radwanski, G. (1970). Polite sit-in: Anti-poverty group wins at city
hall. *The Montreal Gazette* (July): 73.

Ristock, J.L. (1991). Feminist collectives: The struggles in our quest
for a "uniquely feminist structure." In J.D. Wine and J.L.
Ristock (Eds.), *Women and social change: Feminist activism in
Canada* (pp. 41–55). Toronto, ON: Lorimer.

Roseland, M. (1998). *Toward sustainable communities: Resources for
citizens and their governments.* Gabriola Island, BC: New Society
Publishers.

Rothman, J. (1974). Three models of community organization
practice. In F. Cox, J.L. Erlich, J. Rothman, and J. Tropman
(Eds), *Strategies of community organization: A book of readings*
(pp. 22–39). Itasca, IL: F.E. Peacock.

Rothman, J. (1999A). A very personal account of the intellectual history
of community organization. In J. Rothman (Ed.), *Reflections on
community organization: Enduring themes and critical issues*
(pp. 215–34). Itasca, IL: F.E. Peacock.

Rothman, J. (1999B). Historical context in community intervention. In
J. Rothman (Ed.), *Reflections on community organization: Enduring
themes and critical issues* (pp. 27–49). Itasca, IL: F.E. Peacock.

Rubin, H.J., and Rubin, I.S. (1992). *Community organizing and
community development.* 2nd ed. New York, NY: Macmillan.

Shragge, E. (1990). Community based practice: Political alternatives
or new state forms? In L. Davies and E. Shragge (Eds.),
Bureaucracy and community (pp. 137–73). Montreal, QC:
Black Rose Books.

Shragge, E. (1994). Anti-poverty movements: Strategies and
approaches. *City Magazine* 15, 2/3: 27–29.

Shragge, E. (Ed.). (1997). *Community economic development: In search of
empowerment.* Montreal, QC: Black Rose Books.

Shragge, E., and Deniger, M-A. (1997). Quebec's workfare programs: Whose interests? In E. Shragge (Ed.), *Workfare: An ideology for a new underclass* (pp. 17–34). Toronto, ON: Garamond Press.

Shragge, E., and Fontan, J-M. (Eds.). (2000). *Social economy: International debates and perspectives*. Montreal, QC: Black Rose Books.

Starr, A. (2000). *Naming the enemy: Anti-corporate movements confront globalization*. Annandale, NSW: Pluto Press: London: Zed Books.

Stout, L. (1996). *Bridging the class divide and other lessons for grassroots organizing*. Boston, MA: Beacon Press.

Stoecker, R. (2001). Community development and community organizing: Apples and oranges? Chicken and egg? http://comm.org.utoledo.edu/papers.htm

Sturgeon, N. (1995). Theorizing movements: Direct action and direct theory. In M. Darnovsky, B. Epstein, and R. Flacks (Eds.), *Cultural politics and social movements* (pp. 35–51). Philadelphia, PA: Temple University Press.

Swack, M. (1992). Community economic development: An alternative to traditional development. Mimeo.

Swift, J. (1999). *Civil society in question*. Toronto, ON: Between the Lines.

Teodori, M. (Ed.). (1969). *The New Left: A documentary history*. New York, NY: Bobbs-Merrill.

Torjman, S. (1997). *Civil society: Reclaiming our humanity*. Ottawa, ON: Caledon Institute of Social Policy.

United Nations Secretary General. (1955). *Social progress through community development*. New York, NY: United Nations Bureau of Social Affairs.

White, D. (1997). Contradictory participation: Reflections on community action in Quebec. In B. Wharf and M. Clague (Eds.), *Community organizing: Canadian experiences* (pp. 62–90). Toronto, ON: Oxford University Press.

Z Magazine. (2000). A simple plan. *Z Magazine* 13, 2 (February): 6–7.

INDEX

"green" businesses, 126
ideology of, 33–34
"liberal" and "progressive," 125
need to highlight social processes,
    143–44
and neo-liberal ideology, 142
as para-governmental
    organizations, 33, 126
part of social justice movement, 141
problems with, 128–29
relationship with governments, 33,
    52, 57, 126–27, 129–31, 144–45,
    147
reproducing small business model,
    52, 140
short term, 146
stability, 147
strategy to reduce poverty, 129
as vehicle for social change, 129
community gardens, 152, 193
community identity or coherence, 122
community land trusts, 125
community movement.
    See community organizing
community organizations, 184
    autonomy, 51, 55, 114
    democracy, 203
    funding, 32, 55, 57
    legacy of social action, 132
    and oppositional culture, 199–200
    possibilities for renewal, 73, 185
    professionalization, 31–32, 51, 57
    promoting wider changes, 136
    representation and advocacy, 31–32
    resistance to cutbacks, 132
    state policies and, 31–32, 49, 51, 55,
        72–73, 122 (*See also* community
        economic development (CEDs))
community organizing, 16–17, 27, 30,
    34, 67, 97, 159
    autonomy (1960s and 1970s), 44
    conflict model, 66
    definition, 41–43
    delegation of power and roles, 30
    as force for social change, 151
    funding, 19–21 (*See also*
        government funding)
    historical development, 39–40,
        43–59
    legacies, 75–76
    legitimacy in the profession, 14

limits and possibilities, 36
long-term commitment, 96
loss of critical edge, 10, 57, 105
models, 39, 68–73
as opposition, 11, 37, 41
political education, 157
professionalization, 36, 56
radical democracy, 85
redefined, 31
relation to wider issues, 151,
    156–57
representation and advocacy, 51
role of organizers, 21–24, 92
as source of social change, 66,
    196–97
*Community Organizing and Community
    Development* (Rubin and Rubin),
    41, 43
community partnership.
    See partnerships
community sector. *See* community
    organizations
community/union organizers.
    See organizers
Company of Young Canadians (CYC),
    92
Complex G (Quebec City), 181
Comprehensive Community
    Initiatives (CCI), 118
conflict theories, 66, 70–71
consciousness-raising, 99, 105, 148,
    196–97, 202. *See also* education
consensus-building, 66, 69, 109, 198
consensus decision-making, 27–28,
    102
cooperatives, 125
"counter-institutions," 92
credit unions, 126
crisis of work, 117.
    See also unemployment
Cruise missile testing, 25

"de-responsibilized" national
    government, 119
demobilization, 57–58, 82
democracy, 19, 23, 42, 62, 134, 138,
    149, 196, 198
    all aspects of society, 88
    challenges to parliamentary
        democracy, 28

divide and rule, 146
move into community organizing,
92
retreat of, 111
serving corporate interests, 160
government funding, 44, 51, 57
government programs
moved to voluntary sector, 131
grassroots organizing, 32–33, 161
limits and possibilities, 18, 36
Greater Montreal Anti-Poverty and
Coordinating Committee.
See GMAPCC
Gutierrez, L.M., 65, 198

Hasson, S., 43
Hayden, Tom, 91
Homan, M., 110, 118
home care services
CED projects, 130
new "social economy," 130
human capital. See social capital
human chain (demonstration), 25–26

identity politics, 50, 110, 188
moving beyond, 189
Immigrant Workers' Centre (IWC),
190–92
informal links with anti-
globalization activists, 201
immigrants, 50, 159
current experiences of, 179
immigrant labour, 154, 191
organizing, 152
The Importance of History and Context in
Community Organization (Fisher),
72
"In and Against the State" (pamphlet),
145
Industrial Areas Foundation (IAF), 78
Institute for Management and
Community Development
Summer Institute, 179
integration/action, 199
integration/development, 198
integration/opposition, 198
integration strategies, 196–97
intentionality, 199
interests, 113–14
internationalism, 28–29, 94

Jeffery, Susan, 89
job creation, 33
justice agenda, 148

"kitchen meetings," 46
Klein, Naomi, 180
Kovel, J., 199, 202–3
Kretzmann, J.P., 117, 121
Kruzynski, Anna, 45n

labour activism, 154–56. See also trade
union movement
Labour Standards Act (Quebec), 191
Lagassé, Jean, 108
Laxer, James, 86
leadership, 92
Alinsky style, 81
building of, 96, 171
impact of feminism and anti-racism,
65
Learning in Social Action (Foley), 134
Lemert, C., 60
Let the People Decide (Fisher), 90
Levy, Andrea, 189
Lewis, E., 65, 198
Ley, D., 43
liberal feminism, 98
Local Initiative Program grants, 44
local issues
relation to global concerns, 11, 22,
28, 64, 154, 156–57, 186, 192
localism
inherent constraints of, 79
limits of, 80, 93
locality development model, 70–73,
75, 107, 196
support for status quo, 69
Lotz, Jim, 107–9, 203
low-cost housing, 33

mainstreaming, 100
Manji, Irshad, 188
Marcuse, Herbert, 86
Marxism, 66, 84, 93, 95
Marxist-Leninist movement (Quebec)
authoritarianism, 22–23
Mayer, R., 56–57
McGill University, 13–14, 16
McKnight, John, 111, 116–17, 119–21
criticism of, 122
McPhail, M., 99